RICHat26

RICHat26

How I became financially free by twenty-six years old

By Alexis Assadi

I would like to thank everyone with whom I've worked or done business. You've taught me an enormous amount and given me what I needed to write this. I'd also like to thank my partner, Angus, for giving me advice regardless of when or what time I called. Thank you, as well, to Darren for mentoring me and opening up a world of opportunities, and to Roya, Pepper and my parents for everything you've done for me. Lastly, thank you to my wife, Elisa, for your endless support. I dedicate this book to the parents and brother of my dearest friend, Joel, who was tragically killed in an airplane accident in 2011. I wish he was here to see this.

You Should Read This Paragraph

Since this is a book about money, my attorneys require me to include this: I'm not a lawyer, accountant, business consultant, financial advisor or any other kind of professional. I am simply a businessman and investor who learned through trial and error, and therefore I'm not recommending anything to you. Instead, I'm sharing my story. You can take from it as you choose and hopefully there are some useful nuggets of information here. But consult your own team and advisors before making any business or investment decisions. There's also apparently a legal concept called implied fiduciary duty, whereby even though I've told you that I'm not your advisor, you will still consider me to be so. Don't do that please—lawsuits are expensive.

CONTENTS

FOREWORD

There is no magic involved in wealth creation. It's a game of perseverance, positive thinking, dedication and an acute focus on asset accumulation. It's about entrepreneurship, creativity, investing and breaking barriers. Anyone with an imagination, a strong work ethic and a willingness to learn can do it.

Rich At 26 is a pure expression of this. Alexis is proof that a commitment to the craft of achieving financial freedom can yield astonishing results, and that it's possible at any age.

Don't be afraid to challenge the status quo. I made my first million years ago and have made many more since then. Believe me when I say that thinking differently is paramount to creating the financial future you desire.

Darren Weeks

Rich Dad Advisor and
Founder of the Fast Track Group of Companies

PREFACE

I was never interested in money until I turned 19 years old. Until then, I hadn't thought much about it. It's not that I didn't want to have nice things or to be wealthy—it just wasn't something that I contemplated.

One warm afternoon in the summer of 2007 I received a phone call from a woman at the bank. I remember answering the phone and sitting down on a red chair in my sister's room in my parents' home. The lady had called to inquire if I'd considered planning for my financial future. She explained the benefits of saving early for retirement. She told me that if I started to set some money aside today and invested it wisely, over the years I would accumulate enough to retire comfortably.

At the time, I hadn't considered it at all. It didn't even cross my mind. At 19 my life revolved around five interests: girls, music, friends, video games and working out at the gym. I cared more about my social status and how I looked than anything else. My financial future was completely outside of my purview. As long as I had $20 in my wallet to spend I was content.

I can't recall every detail of my conversation with the banker. But I do remember it ending with my investing in one of her products, a mutual fund. This particular fund was supposedly very safe and conservative—it had never before lost money. She said that if I invested today, it would give me slow, steady growth over the years. I would be able to sleep well at night knowing that my capital would still be there in the morning and would help me retire comfortably.

The mutual fund sounded like a good deal to me. At the time I had a total of $1,000 to my name. I was a university student who only worked part-time, but I invested everything I had into that one product. I also agreed to a regular contribution plan whereby I would invest an additional $25 each month. Over the span of 40 years, the money was supposed to turn into a lot more than what it was currently worth. It might even grow into a million dollars one day if I invested larger amounts in the future. To me, that was a lot of money. It was an exciting idea.

Truthfully, I had no clue about what I was doing. It was only hours ago that I'd woken up without a single thought about investing, and now I suddenly had a portfolio. The term mutual fund was alien to me, but I figured that if the bank was recommending it then it would be a good idea. I mean, a bank always looks out for its clients' interests, right?

Welcome to the World of Money

A few days after buying units in the mutual fund, I realized that the money I invested was no longer in my trusty bank account; it was now in an investment that I didn't control. My hard-earned dollars were in someone else's hands and at the fate of another person's judgement. The banker had said the mutual fund was safe, but was it? I felt as though one wrong decision could mean that I would lose everything.

To make matters worse, I didn't even know who the person handling my money was or what he or she was doing with it. Where was my money going? What was I investing in? What the heck was a mutual fund, anyway? A panicky feeling swept over me. One thousand dollars was my life's savings and I didn't want to lose it.

It soon dawned on me that I should learn about what was happening to my cash. If I could understand what I invested in, perhaps I could protect it. In order to learn more, I began to read financial publications and acquaint myself with the world of money. It felt like learning a new language. At 19, I was a political science student and had never been exposed to finance. I hadn't ever stepped foot into the business school on campus, let alone taken a course in commerce or economics.

In spite of my inexperience, I started to learn by buying magazines like Forbes, The Economist and Canadian Business, and by reading the business section on news websites. The articles were complex and intimidating. On the bus ride to class I would browse through the Wall Street Journal app on my BlackBerry and read about unfamiliar companies like ExxonMobil and Pfizer. The sums of money discussed were enormous to the point that I couldn't comprehend them. A billion dollars, which is to multiply a million dollars one thousand times, was completely outside of my mental scope.

Unbeknown to me then, the phone call with the banker changed my life forever. Had she not tried to sell me a mutual fund, perhaps I would never have become interested in investing. The simple act of risking my hard-earned capital compelled me to absorb everything I could about money. I wanted to understand it all so that I could protect my investment. As time passed, I became more experienced, invested more money and continued to learn. I graduated to reading more advanced publications and was less intimidated by the financial lexicon; the more I learned, the better an investor I became. And the more money I invested, the more I was compelled to keep learning...

RICH AT 26

RICH AT 26

As you probably guessed from the title, I got rich at the age of 26. To be clear, when I say rich I mean that I had built enough wealth to never need to work again. I had an investment portfolio that paid enough passive income to allow me to live the life of my choice. I made more money from my assets than most people earn from their jobs. In short, I was financially free.

In my early 20s I made investments because I wanted to be wealthy when I got older. Today, however, at the grand age of 27 I do it because I love it. I own a venture capital company, Assadi Global Ventures, which I use to finance budding entrepreneurs. I love investing because it allows me to do good while adding to my own wealth. It's a constant win-win. If I can create jobs, finance new technologies or help increase people's quality of life – and make money doing it – I'm a very happy camper.

While I don't give financial advice or consider myself a role model, I am an example of someone who made a lot of money doing the opposite of what is traditionally recommended. I don't save, I don't have a retirement account, I don't listen to financial advisors and I don't own my house. In fact, I can't think of anything I do that falls in line with what the professionals recommend.

I wrote this book to add a different perspective to the personal finance conversation. Everything I did to build my wealth was unconventional and unlike what most others do. However, since "most others" aren't wealthy, I also believe that breaking away from the mould makes a lot of sense. When it comes to money, being like everyone else means living pay cheque to pay cheque.

I'll preface the rest of this book by saying that I'm not out to attack bankers, financial advisors or anyone else in that industry. But aside from using bank accounts, credit cards and loans to finance investments, I don't really use any of their services. Once in a blue moon I might buy a stock, but in general I steer clear from what financial institutions offer. In my opinion, their investment and insurance products are for people who are financially lazy. They don't want to take the time to manage their own wealth; they'd rather have others do it for them. Instead of searching for great investments, they'd rather contribute $100 a month to a bank-managed mutual fund.

Unfortunately, society in general is lackadaisical when it comes to wealth management. People's apathy towards their own finances has created a massively profitable void for banks, mutual fund companies, insurers and industry professionals to fill. They offer everything from bank accounts, insurance policies, estate planning, investment services, loans, mortgages and debt consolidation plans – all designed to help shape your financial future.

While it may be common knowledge, this fact is clearly not absorbed by most: financial services companies are businesses. They have shareholders who demand performance. As such, with their products come steep fees and juicy commissions which often eradicate the returns for the client. Once the firm, its shareholders and employees get paid – then the customer can benefit. Assuming, of course, that there's anything left. To be frank about it, most financial institutions put their needs first and ours last. I think the subprime meltdown just a few years ago illustrated that perfectly.

Why You Need to Take Ownership of Your Wealth

2008 and 2009 were the worst economic times in recent history. For years prior, Americans had taken out unaffordable mortgages with no money down to purchase homes. They relied on rising wages, healthy employment and national prosperity to continue and thus float their lifestyles. Nations across the world also encumbered dangerous levels of debt, further menacing an already intertwined global economy.

Predictably, a world financed on credit could only last for so long. In 2008 thousands of Americans began to default on their mortgage payments, triggering a series of chain reactions that led to an international catastrophe. Many of their mortgages had been collateralized into investable products and were sold to clients as safe investments. They were also underwritten and insured by multi-billion dollar institutions.

Widespread mortgage defaults caused liquidity to evaporate, companies to collapse and left millions unemployed. As jobs were shed, people who could previously afford their mortgage payments and lifestyles fell into ruin, further escalating the crisis. Banks and insurers crumbled, stocks plummeted and millions across the world were left penniless. Trillions of dollars were lost and we narrowly avoided re-entrance into the Stone Age. As this book goes to press in 2015, many nations still haven't fully recovered from the calamity.

In the following years society defiled bankers for their involvement in the global meltdown. Financial institutions were "evil" and the well-intended, poorly-informed Occupy Wall Street movement began. Our outrage was exacerbated when we learned that institutions not only sold bad investments, but also bet against them knowing that their clients would suffer. Legislation was soon passed to restructure the way the financial markets operated and the industry as a whole was harangued for its unscrupulousness. Bankers should not have allowed (or convinced) their clients to assume outrageous amounts of debt. They shouldn't have been undercapitalized and susceptible to so much risk. They shouldn't have lied, cheated or stolen and they absolutely should not have sold toxic investments for their own financial gain.

While the above is all true – bankers did act disgustingly – society placed little blame on its own shoulders. For example, while banks should not have given risky loans, their clients shouldn't have taken them either. Nobody was coerced at gunpoint to do so. People made poor decisions and bankers took advantage of it. The same goes for selling bad investments. While they should have never been sold, people took their advisors at their word without performing proper due diligence and paid the price for it.

In my mind, what happened in 2008 is not about what's right or wrong. Yes, I wish more bankers had not been slime balls. I wish more of them truly cared for their clients. I wish that the entire system was different. I also wish that my lawyers didn't overbill me and that we can one day have world peace. But that is never going to happen.

The reality is that our widespread lack of financial intelligence is ultimately to blame. Had we better understood how to make investments and manage our money, would we have blindly bought toxic assets from investment advisors? Would we have tried to purchase a home when we couldn't afford one? Would we have allowed the system to morph into an unregulated wild west commandeered by cowboy Wall Street financiers? If society took the time to educate itself about money, would the Great Recession ever have happened? Let's leave issues of morality to philosophers and discuss what things are actually like.

The truth is that we as a people are senseless when it comes to money. It's not taught in school, it's taboo to talk to your friends about wealth and we take little ownership of our own financial affairs. Instead, we take our "advice" from bankers and mutual fund companies who make a living by selling us their high-commission low-performance products. And then we wonder why it's so hard to get rich. Even worse, we wonder how and why financial institutions burned us!

Our anger should not be pointed towards the financial services industry. They wouldn't sell their products if we didn't buy them. Instead, we should be furious at ourselves. Why are we so uneducated about money? Why have we allowed this to continue for centuries? Why did we congratulate presidents like Bill Clinton and George W. Bush for making it easier for people to afford homes? Why do we obsess over race, religion, sex, gender, immigration, drugs and war, but never hold a broad conversation about our wealth management?

Conclusion

What happened in 2008 is only a microcosm of our disastrous financial management. I could rattle off a hundred statistics to depict the state of people's circumstances: high debt, low incomes, no assets, unemployment, underemployment – you name it. But as I see it, we have nobody but ourselves to blame. If more people took control of their finances, if they took their investment portfolios as seriously as they do watching sports on TV, then perhaps we wouldn't be in this position.

A lot of people want to know how I made my money. Most of my readers are in their 20s and 30s and want to know my "secret." So here it is: I learned how to do it. I took action, surrounded myself with people who were not only rich, but who got rich in a way that I wanted to emulate, and I copied them. I took their advice, analysed their decisions and did everything I possibly could to invest in my financial education. I relied on myself; not on industry professionals. I took control of my finances and lo and behold, I made a lot of money in a few short years.

If there's only one point to grasp from my book, it's this: the best way to create wealth, protect against loss and become financially free is to learn about money. Getting rich isn't hard, but it does take effort and discipline. Take it seriously and view yourself as a professional. In the same way that lawyers, doctors and accountants study for years before they can practice, invest your time into mastering your craft. You will quite literally get back what you put in - trust me on that.

Rich At 26 is not meant to show you what to do to become a millionaire. Rather, it's to demonstrate that it is very possible for a young person to build a lot of wealth in today's economic climate. My hope is that this book contributes in some way to your financial education. I'm probably not right about everything and I'm surely wrong about some things, but I hope that what I have to add benefits you in some way.

I GOT RICH IN MY 20s.
HERE'S HOW YOU CAN TOO

I GOT RICH IN MY 20s.
HERE'S HOW YOU CAN TOO

There's a common misconception that people can't really become wealthy until they reach their middle-age. With the hindrance of backbreaking debts and little life experience, 20 or 30-something year-olds should instead focus on learning and aim to "move up." Once they reach their 40s they'll have made a career for themselves. They'll have also paid down their debts, accumulated some savings and can begin to plan for retirement.

Of course, I know this to be false because of my own situation. But, at first glance, many believe that I built my wealth because of anomalies: I must have gotten lucky or perhaps my father knew the right people. I went to private school so I must have had help somewhere along the line. Or maybe I did something special that others would find hard to replicate. Regardless, getting rich at 26 is next to impossible for most people.

The reality is in fact quite the opposite. While I had loving parents and a good upbringing, neither had connections that could help me in business. My dad was a diplomat who spent his career in Asia and my mother spent most of hers caring for my sister and I. Moreover, I didn't strike gold or win the lottery. I didn't have a major breakthrough that turned me into an overnight millionaire. Aside from committing myself to my craft, I did nothing special at all.

What Kind of Wealth Do I Have?

Being rich does not entail having a lot of cash in the bank. Instead, it requires having assets that produce cash. For example, real estate, businesses, employees, investments, etc. Understanding that concept completely changed my life. If you can grasp it, I guarantee that it will for you as well.

With that said, I don't have a mountain of cash. If you look in my bank account you won't see $10 million. Instead, I own a portfolio of assets that pay me a consistent income – to the point that I earn more from them than most jobs could pay. Each month I can drain my accounts because I know that the next month my assets will produce more cash for me to spend. I will never again need to rely on employment to live a good life.

By this point you may be wondering whether I'm a frugal, penny-pinching minimalist. It would probably be easier to claim you're financially free if you live with 12 roommates and have monthly expenses of $150. Without delving into my personal life I will say that that is not the case. I obviously don't spend recklessly, but

I live in a good part of town, travel frequently, buy nice things and eat at expensive restaurants. I have guilty pleasures and most of them cost money.

In fact, building wealth has little to do with reducing expenses and everything with acquiring assets. More assets equals more income, and more income means a greater ability to spend. That's why I cringe when I see authors and bloggers recommending that you cut up your credit cards, shop at discount stores, clip coupons and basically live like a pauper. I never did that.

How I Got Started

Like most young people, I got a job in my early 20s and earned an average income from it. I made roughly what any 23 year-old could expect to make with an undergraduate degree in political science. With each paycheque I received, after paying bills I was able to squirrel away a couple of hundred dollars.

However, contrary to most, I did not save the money. Since wealth is built by acquiring assets, that's what I chose to do. Instead of keeping the cash in my bank account, I invested it. Specifically, I made investments that paid a monthly income. That's in contrast with ones that realize profits through a price increase.

Now, it's important to note that my first investments were not good ones. I was neither experienced nor informed enough to know much about what I was doing. Thus, to begin with, I bought income-producing mutual funds (bond funds, for example) that paid an annualized cash flow of around 3%. Each month I would put a portion of my paycheque into one of those funds, and the next month the investment would dump a few dollars back into my bank account.

Rather than spend it, I would reinvest that extra income along with whatever I could scrape from my paycheque. It was a simple process that I repeated for several months. Here's an example of what it might have looked like:

January:
invest $500

February:
invest $500 + the $2
I earned from last month's investment

March:
invest $500 + the $2.10
that I earned from last month's investment

April:
invest $500 + the $2.20
that I earned from last month's investment

Becoming More Advanced:
The Spitfire Approach

As you could imagine, doing the above would take forever to build meaningful wealth. Fortunately, with practice I became a better investor. As I gained experience, over time I graduated from mutual funds to stocks. I began to buy shares in Real Estate Investment Trusts (REITs), Mortgage Investment Corporations (MICs) and income-producing assets that paid substantially more than 3% per year. I found ones that produced 8,9 and 10% and placed my capital in those. And I continued to add money from my paycheques each month.

As math would have it, buying higher-yielding assets caused my investment income to escalate from a few dollars a month to a few-dozen dollars. It was at that point that my portfolio then began to snowball.

Knowing that I lacked the capital to generate large cash returns, my investment strategy was to capitalize on compounding growth. Rather than waiting for my assets to rise over the long term (i.e. buying a stock low and selling it high) and potentially reinvesting only once or twice a year, I chose to take small, quick income injections and reinvest them monthly. Thus, I could compound my growth multiple times annually.

Rudimentary math will explain why I chose my particular investing strategy: the power of compounding growth is astonishing. For example, imagine that you invested $10 million for a period of ten years, and received a return of 10% per year. If you were to reinvest your returns only once a year, your capital would be worth $25,937,424.60 after a decade. However, compounding it monthly would equate to $27,070,414.91 - nearly a $2 million difference. To me, it was a no-brainer: invest and reinvest as frequently as possible.

While I didn't start with much, it didn't take long for my portfolio to begin pumping out a couple of hundred dollars each month. Eventually, I earned enough income from it to make investments not just every 30 days, but bi-weekly. At this point, the power of compounding interest doubled - and you can probably guess where this is headed. Soon I earned enough passive income to make small investments on a weekly basis, further accelerating the rate that my income compounded. Yet, this was only the beginning.

Becoming Sophisticated

There's a chapter in this book called How to Make Super Low Risk, Very High Return Investments. In short, I stress that investing is like any other profession: it requires dedicating a huge portion of your life to learning, studying and becoming an expert. Those who are truly sophisticated are able to make investments with no risk that still pump out enormous returns.

Over the years I eventually became a sophisticated investor. This was the single most crucial development to getting rich in my 20s. Instead of earning single or low double-digit returns, I was able to generate multiples more than what I used to receive.

If you take away only one point from this chapter, it should be this: I became a sophisticated investor because I learned from rich people who got wealthy through investing. A result of persistence and networking, by the age of 23 I found myself in an environment of inconceivably wealthy businesspeople. Some were real estate developers, others were oilmen, technology entrepreneurs and healthcare pioneers. My mentor, for example, owns 5,000 apartment units and a couple of cruise ports. One of his friends has nearly double that real estate.

Instead of being caged in a corporate environment that fosters good employees, I inhabited one that promotes entrepreneurship and investment prowess. Rather than learning from financial advisors who get rich by selling investment products, I learned from rich people who actually got rich from investing. Regardless of education or formal training, these people were multi-millionaires and are the true experts in wealth creation. And as any person would, I soaked it up like a sponge.

For instance, the first thing I learned is that rich people think differently about money. They acquire assets and don't hunt for cash. As a result, while most hope to be employees with big salaries, rich people strive to own employees. They buy businesses - and if they can't be bought, they build them. If an employee is earning six-figures you can bet your bottom dollar that the business owners are making much more than that.

Second, I learned that there are oceans of mouth-watering investments out there. Literally, it's like a sea of money waiting to be snorkeled in. However, finding, analyzing and investing in them takes more than clicking a button in your online brokerage. You can't just look them up on Google Finance. In fact, the best and most lucrative investments are often not publicly-traded, meaning that you can't buy them through your broker. They are private enterprises owned by entrepreneurs. To be blunt about it, stocks and mutual funds are second-class investments made for unsophisticated investors. It's extremely difficult for a retail investor to do well in the markets.

Now, it's around this point when people frequently ask, "Well, what about people like Warren Buffett and billionaire fund managers who got rich from trading stocks?" They wonder how I have the gall to even suggest that when the richest man in the world is a stock trader. However, this is a misinformed question. People like Warren Buffett didn't get wealthy by putting their money in the markets and trading their way to riches. Instead, they got rich by managing other people's money and charging fees to do so. They created investment funds, convinced clients to buy into them and then charged fees for their services.

They are business owners, and investment management is their business.

Sadly, entrepreneurship gets a bad rap. The word "risky" hangs around its neck like a tombstone. It is seen as a huge risk, huge return game largely thanks to today's media. Journalists and bloggers prefer to report on the glamour of the technology entrepreneur who became an overnight billionaire in his basement. They ignore the other 99% of the industry as though it doesn't exist.

The truth is that there is a mean between extremes. Some businesses come with stomach-churning risk and others are home-run opportunities. Some are in between. The risk profile largely depends on economic conditions and management ability. The trick is to have the skill set to know which deals are investable.

Thanks to my surroundings I was able to acquire those skills. I learned to accurately gauge the potential for a successful investment and also to ask for help when I needed it. I gained access to a network of partners who were experts in their respective fields, be it real estate, energy, law, accounting, banking, credit, etc. I also received tremendous deal flow from my network; on a weekly basis new investment opportunities became available.

Thus, rather than investing in stocks and mutual funds, I put my cash into these private investments. I invested in secured loans, real estate and a range of small businesses. If I didn't have the money to invest, I waited a couple of months until I could come up with more capital. My wealth soared almost overnight.

Increasing My Buying Power

As I alluded to in the previous paragraph, I didn't always have the money to make investments. While my asset base was growing rapidly, there was a never-ending train of lucrative opportunities that I simply couldn't afford to finance.

Rather than missing out on those deals, I decided to raise capital for them. Specifically, I borrowed money to make investments: literally hundreds of thousands of dollars. Of course, I started with small amounts and gradually increased it. As I gained experience I became comfortable with managing investment debt and took on more.

Each time I took a loan, I invested the capital and made a profit by keeping the difference between the rate of return and what I owed the lender. For example, say I borrowed $100,000 at an interest rate of 7%. I would then invest it and earn 18%. Once I got the money back, I would repay the lender the $100,000, plus the $7,000 in interest - and keep the $11,000 profit. Of course, I reinvested the profit into new deals.

Obviously, using this kind of leverage comes with a lot of risk if done incorrectly. But that takes us back to my original point: sophisticated investors are the ones that get wealthy. For me, the result was an explosion of growth. The combination of borrowing money to invest and putting it into extremely profitable projects is ultimately what sealed the deal. By my mid-20s I was rich, earning more investment income than most make in a lifetime.

The Art of Raising Capital, by Darren Weeks, is a great read for those who want to pursue this avenue.

Conclusion

What I hope to have impressed upon you is that getting rich in your 20s is certainly viable. However, it does require a different perspective on money and investing. It also takes effort. If you're pursuing wealth I believe that you need to do two things:

First, understand that you must acquire assets that pay you income. If you can't afford to buy those assets, create them. You get rich from owning businesses and investments – nothing else. That simple concept made me realize that being an employee and saving money is not the road to riches. That's the first step, and it's one that most people don't grasp.

Second, associate yourself with people who built their wealth from business and investing. Network, find mentors and get acquainted with those from whom you can learn. They exist in every community, online and offline – the trick is to find them. Whether you're Googling "[insert city] entrepreneurs," attending wealth-building seminars, joining local small business organizations or reading your favorite blogs and websites, there are plenty of resources out there. Invest in your financial intelligence and work towards becoming a sophisticated investor. Learn how to get rich from people who are already rich – and make sure they built their wealth in a way that you want to emulate. I can't stress that enough. The sooner your network includes them the faster you'll progress.

THE ULTIMATE GUIDE TO BUILDING WEALTH WHEN YOU'RE SHORT ON CASH

THE ULTIMATE GUIDE TO BUILDING WEALTH WHEN YOU'RE SHORT ON CASH

The universal question about investing, business and wealth creation is, "How can I do it when I don't have any money?" Whether you're 17 years old and want to get started or 45, divorced and bankrupt, it's an issue that just about everyone faces. At least 90% of my readers' questions revolve around this topic.

The fact is that it's much easier to make money when you already have lots of it. That's why the rich get richer while most others stagnate. Even a mere 5% return on $1 million is $50,000; a big chunk of cash for anyone. So if you're starting out with nothing, you should know from the get-go that it's going to be an uphill battle. As investment giant Charles Munger once put it, "The first $100,000 is a b!@#$."

In this chapter I'll outline three solutions to creating wealth while you have little to no money. The theme throughout Rich At 26 is financial intelligence, which is what you'll need to properly execute the strategies below.

Adjust Your Perspective

To understand how to you'll accomplish your goal, you'll need to change your perspective. First, instead of asking, "How do I build wealth when I don't have any money?," adjust it to this: "What resources can I use to acquire assets?" As you know, wealth is simply a matter of accumulating investments and businesses. If you acquire enough of them you'll become financially free.

Second, realize that money – cash – is only a tool. It's something that you can use to acquire the assets you want. However, it is neither the only tool out there, nor is it the most efficient or least risky. It just happens to be the most convenient. So take a moment to consider which other resources are at your disposal. What other methods of acquisition can you use to capture an asset? Are you good at something that others would pay to learn about? Do you have a skill or a trade that you excel at? Could you turn your knowledge, connections or relationships into a business?

Solution #1: Create Deals for Other Investors

One of the best ways to build wealth is to help others do it, too, by creating great investments for them. This is a strategy often employed by entrepreneurs who want to buy real estate without using their own money. Instead of using their capital, they create real estate investments for other people and participate in the profits. They provide a service to those who want to invest in property but aren't interested or skilled in collecting rent, fixing toilets and dealing with tenants. The investors are passive; they want the profits but not the problems. And therein lies the potential for a perfect partnership. Here's how it often works:

The entrepreneur finds a lucrative piece of real estate that can be invested in. He has enough knowledge to be confident that the property, the market and the economy are all conducive to profit. With the help of a lawyer, realtor and banker he can create the legal entity, accounts and other administrative amenities to accommodate the asset's acquisition. The entrepreneur is responsible for every "active" element of the investment, including managing the property, renovating and maintaining it, collecting rent, finding and screening tenants and ultimately ensuring that it's a fruitful venture.

The investor, on the other hand, is only required as a capital partner. He simply invests his cash and in some cases also is used to secure the mortgage. He has no involvement in the management of the real estate.

Since both partners are required for the opportunity to be successful, they split the profits. While the entrepreneur couldn't have purchased the property without the investor's money, the investor wouldn't have had access to the deal without the entrepreneur, especially not passively.

In fact, depending on the entrepreneur's experience and track record, it isn't uncommon for him to receive more than half of the net earnings. There are some who charge an up-front fee for the investor to even be involved in the deal!

Of course, buying real estate with other people's money is just an example. Similar models can be used for just about any venture. I've been approached with everything from plain-vanilla house flipping to advertising billboards and farming bee hives – there's nothing that's too weird or out of the box to be invested in. There are passive investors like me all over the world waiting for entrepreneurs like you to create great deals for us to both profit through. If you don't have money to invest, do you have a venture that you're confident would be successful if you had a capital partner?

Now, I should note that raising capital from investors requires an entirely new set of skills. It involves finding, approaching and ultimately selling your idea to people who have funds to invest. There are also legal guidelines that govern from whom and how you can raise money. Don't attempt to do so without exploring how to first.

Solution #2: Borrow Money to Invest

If you prefer to be a passive investor and not an active entrepreneur, you can still do so without your own cash. Instead, you can use credit, which is money borrowed from a lender (banks, etc.). By securing a loan with an attractive interest rate and term you can purchase assets that you otherwise couldn't afford

For example, if you borrowed $20,000 at 5% interest and made 10% on your investment – after repaying the lender you'd earn a $1,000 profit. In many places you'd even receive tax benefits for doing this.

Of course, along with the benefit of leverage come the risks associated with failure. If you borrow money and make an unsuccessful investment with it, you'll still be required to repay the loan with interest. As well, if your deal doesn't return at least what you're paying in interest, the loan could become an encumbrance. If you're paying 5% in interest but are only earning 2% in profit, your cash flow will be negative. You'll need to find other sources of income to pay what you owe to the lender each month. To guard against this, many people only invest in income-producing assets that will surely return more than the monthly interest rate.

Solution #3:
Start A Business That Can Be Scaled

Most self-made millionaires and billionaires created their wealth by launching a successful business. Done correctly and with a little bit of luck, a business can escalate from a simple idea to a booming enterprise. And thanks to the internet and modern technology, starting one has never been easier or less expensive.

Moreover, once your company generates cash, you can then use it to expand your venture or to invest into other passive deals. A business is a phenomenal way to build an asset because you can virtually create something from nothing.

However, before diving into the first venture that excites you it's important to ensure that it can be scaled. That means that once it's up and running the business should be able to function and grow without you actively managing it. This is a crucial detail. Scaling might entail having employees, licensees, independent salespeople or online commerce. A well-leveraged company should be able to make money whether or not you're working on it. If it doesn't scale you could find yourself in the same position as many small business owners: working 24/7 on a company that you can never get away from.

For example, starting a consulting company that relies solely on your experiences is difficult to leverage because it's all about you. Instead, think of ventures that involve products and services which can be used at the same time by many customers.

Also note that a non-scalable business is far less attractive to potential buyers and partners, thus reducing the avenues from which you can profit. You should start a business with the intent to sell it, even if you don't ever plan on doing so.

In a similar vein, you could also consider creating a product that requires an investment of your time and expertise, but not of your capital. A perfect example is this book. While writing Rich At 26 took hundreds of hours, plenty of frustration and personal sacrifice, it didn't require much cash up-front. After hiring an editor and graphic designer and paying for an ISBN code, there were no other costs. Since I have a website with a large readership I also don't need a publisher or distributor. And I only pay for each physical book when I receive an order, meaning that I'm never in a negative cash position.

Thus, after putting in a considerable amount of effort, this book became an asset. And since it's mainly sold through AlexisAssadi.net, it turned my website into one, too.

Conclusion

Unfortunately, when it comes to business and investing there are no shortcuts. There's no secret remedy that will catapult you to wealth in 24 hours. It is certainly harder to make money when you don't have much to work with. However, remember that your objective must be to accumulate assets. Using cash to do this is only one option. Your creativity and ability to use the resources at your fingertips can be much more powerful tools.

HOW TO MAKE
SUPER LOW RISK,
VERY HIGH RETURN
INVESTMENTS

HOW TO MAKE SUPER LOW RISK, VERY HIGH RETURN INVESTMENTS

The greatest lie ever told to the common investor is that to earn a higher return, she needs to take on more risk. If she wants to grow her capital considerably, there must be some uncertainty. In fact, to call this a 'lie' doesn't do justice to the depths of its reach. A lie describes an untruth; a mere spec of dishonesty. Like telling someone you're 34 when you're really 40, it's not a big deal and it probably won't cause much harm.

However, the idea that high-risk equals high-return is more than that. It's a falsity that is today a universal concept. It has percolated, like a nasty wart, from the annals of Wall Street brokerages to the desks of financial advisors, on the screens of readers' computers and ultimately to the common investor. To call it a lie would be like calling the plague the common cold: an enormous understatement.

Instead, high-risk equals high-return is a legend. It's a dark, vile and walloping myth that has existed for centuries. It's one that has caused hundreds of millions of unsuspecting investors to take unnecessary risks - and risks that they couldn't afford - and many suffered because of it. Most importantly, it's a legend that's just not true.

Un-excitingly, this myth is not propagated by sinister sorcerers bent on financial domination. There are no evil Wall Street barons conspiring to trick the masses for their own personal gain (at least not about this!). Rather, that people believe a high amount of risk must be taken to receive a high return results from a snowball of rampant misinformation, widespread financial illiteracy and the simple fact that most investors are just not sophisticated enough to make informed decisions. The depth of this moronic intrusion is profound and has fooled investors and advisors alike. Today, industry professionals buy into the myth and make recommendations to clients based on it.

How to Make Low-Risk, High-Return Investments

Like most problems in society, debunking the high-risk equals high-return myth requires education. When people get smarter, they typically do better at things. Consider healthcare, for instance. Doctors don't want us to die from heart disease and lung cancer, so they try to educate us about the harms of smoking and eating poorly. Those who receive that education and take action on it have a better chance of being healthy.

The same applies to money. But, unlike health, learning to make investments is not a subject that is taught in school. And even if it was, it most likely would not be taught by the right teachers. The only people, in my opinion, who are qualified to give investment advice are people who got rich from making investments. And they are few and far between. So it's nobody's fault that investors aren't well-informed. Investing is a tough thing to do and there are few people out there who are good at it.

Coincidentally, I happen to be one of those people. I'm not great at much else, but making good investments is something I excel at. It's how I've built my wealth, it's what I do and it's what I write about. And I consistently make outstanding investments with little to no risk involved.

As a sophisticated investor, I can tell you that the trick is not knowing the next hot stock ahead of the others. It doesn't involve intricate techniques only taught in MBA school. To be perfectly honest, I can hardly do long division myself. Instead, being a successful investor requires dedicating a substantial portion of your life to learning about, improving on and honing your craft.

Now, before I sound too righteous I will concede that I've had an unfair advantage. Unlike most others, I live and work in an environment of entrepreneurs, businesspeople and women and men who made their money by investing. Since 23 I've known nothing but people who make outstanding investments - and I've emulated what they do. After several years I picked up a few tricks of the trade. However, my point remains: Learning how to make good investments from people who built their wealth from investing is key to earning great returns without assuming much risk.

A Recent Example

One of the investments I made last year was providing a secured loan to a business partner, and charging interest on it. The borrower needed capital to help finance a real estate deal, so we negotiated the terms and eventually moved forward. I was comfortable lending the money partly because I knew him personally, but also because he earned a salary of around $150,000 per year. As well, he presented a clear plan for how I would recoup my capital. I saw little risk of him missing payments or not being able to return my funds. Thus, I loaned him a six-figure amount at an annual interest rate of 15%. As security for my money, he pledged two pieces of real estate and five personal guarantees.

If you're not familiar with how these kinds of deals work, they essentially go like this: the borrower has my money for a period of time that we both agree on (1 year, 3 years, etc.). Until the repayment date, he needs to make monthly interest payments - in this case, in the amount of 15% per year. If the borrower doesn't make the agreed upon payments or fails to return my capital, I have the legal right to seize two pieces of real estate and sue five people who are all equally liable for the loan (interest, principal, late fees and all). Any legal costs that I incur must also be borne by the defendants.

Where's the Risk?

Because of the collateral that the borrower pledged, there is practically no risk to this investment. In order to lose all my money, the value of both pieces of real estate would need to drop by 70% and all five guarantors would need to die (without assets) or go bankrupt. Yet, at the same time I'm earning 15% per year – an amount most investors would salivate over. I also don't need my money back anytime soon, so there are no liquidity issues.

So what separates this investment from the average Joe's stock or mutual fund? How was I able to do a no risk, high return deal? The answer is financial intelligence. As a sophisticated and well-connected investor, I was able to do a deal where multiple banks, law firms, insurers, realtors and mortgage brokers were involved. Over the course of a month, we analyzed property appraisals and tax assessments, took assets in trust and placed titles on real estate. When all was said and done, 30 or 40 pages of documents were signed.

The average investor quite simply does not have knowledge, experience, relationships or connections to make an investment similar to the one above. In fact, she likely does not know that these kinds of opportunities exist. To her understanding, the only options out there are stocks, bonds and mutual funds – and she's therefore limited to those. If she did want to pursue a deal like the above, she probably would not know where to begin.

Conclusion

Being an investor is no different than being a lawyer, doctor, dentist or accountant – aside from the fact that we don't overcharge for our services (kidding!). Like any other profession, being good requires study, practice, learning and networking. It also entails having a team or community of people who are knowledgeable in areas of expertise that you may lack.

Any sophisticated investor who built her wealth by investing will tell you this: the myth of needing to take steep risks to get a great return is believed by the inexperienced. These are people who are misinformed and are therefore reduced to the investments hocked by banks, brokerages and mutual fund companies. That, unfortunately, is the majority of the population.

Of course, I'm not suggesting that there is no correlation between risk and return. It is certainly true that if you invest in a local tech start-up you could very well hit a home-run or lose all of your money. That's an example of a zero-sum investment. Instead, my point is that there does not have to be a correlation. As such, sophisticated investors are able to find deals where that correlation is either minimal, can be actively mitigated or does not reasonably exist, yet can still yield astronomical returns.

Thus, I implore you to carefully consider the financial advice you receive. Who is actually qualified to make recommendations to you? Does simply passing a test and having a license render a person financially intelligent? Or, should that person have a proven track record of making incredible returns with her own personal investment portfolio? My preference is to learn from those who've done it themselves with their own money.

THE MAMMOTH GUIDE
TO INVESTING
WITH ENTREPRENEURS

THE MAMMOTH GUIDE TO INVESTING WITH ENTREPRENEURS

Most of the wealth I've accumulated came as a result of meeting, learning from and eventually investing with experienced, wealthy entrepreneurs. Rather than placing capital in mutual funds, bonds and stocks, I found private investments with small business owners more attractive. They were often higher-yielding and lower risk, and far superior to the alternatives. They've consistently trumped returns made in the public markets. In fact, I don't think I've bought a stock since 2012.

Debunking the Myth That Investing With Entrepreneurs Is Risky

Many bank-trained portfolio managers will tell you that private investments are hyper-risky. As such, they should only comprise a small portion of your assets – if any. The rest should be a balance of stocks and mutual funds. When most think about entrepreneurs they imagine a pioneering, adventurous, risk-taking enthusiast who will put it all on the line to achieve success. To invest with one would yield only one of two outcomes: you'd either lose it all or make millions.

As exciting as that all sounds, it frankly isn't the case. While the media salivates over founders of companies like Facebook, Whats App, Google and Uber – young, quirky and ingenious adults who created billions nearly overnight – there is a cosmos of unglamorous small business owners with steady, profitable ventures who need capital to expand. In the USA, alone, there are nearly 30 million small companies and they employ close to half the population. Yet, they're practically ignored and seldom considered for investment.

The small business world cannot simply be defined by a blanket statement, like "only invest in private deals if you're willing to lose it all." There is a huge variation of risk, depending on who is running the company, what the business is and what the market is like. Some ventures have a 1% chance of success and others are nearly guaranteed. Companies in the technology space are notoriously risky, as are wildcatting oil drillers. However, certain real estate deals are nearly impossible to fail. Some companies are just ideas, while others are established firms with employees, systems and plenty of revenue. Each business is entirely distinct and it's impossible to generalize the hundreds of millions out there.

In addition to each business being different, each investment opportunity varies as well. For example, a super-safe real estate project can be cannibalized by a bad deal structure. I've seen deals come apart at the seams because they weren't incorporated properly, were highly tax-inefficient and didn't leave enough for the investor. While the asset may have done well, the investors got burned because it was set up amateurishly. I've also seen others that were risky on the surface, but were backed by enough collateral to make it secure.

As I've mentioned before, the solution is to have the ability to find and assess opportunities that are both lucrative and safe - because they do exist. The best deals come with no risk, high returns, plenty of tax benefits and also do good for society. And they are plentiful in the world of entrepreneurs.

7 Reasons to Invest With Entrepreneurs

1. When done correctly, it is possible to eliminate virtually all risk. To attract investors' capital, entrepreneurs are often willing to put up collateral. As a result, it's common for an entrepreneur to pledge his home, vehicles and even have his friends or family personally guarantee the investment. I've done numerous deals where literal widespread death, destruction and bankruptcy would have to occur before my capital was at risk.

2. The profits can be massive. Small businesses implicitly have plenty of room to grow. If you catch the right deal at the right time, your returns could be sky-high. For instance, one of my colleagues invested in a small company that was later purchased by a publicly-traded firm. On that deal, alone, he made millions. However, several years later the acquiring company was bought by Yahoo and his investment multiplied again. While it's hard to calculate a true ROI, it was likely somewhere in the ballpark of 10,000%.

3. The profits can be much higher than average. Now that I mentioned the above, I should also be more realistic. Chances are that you won't invest in a private firm before it goes public. While it's true that a small business can be bought and investors can make millions, more often the deals are less glamorous. Personally, I've only ever invested in one deal that yielded over triple-digit returns. However, I've participated in many that pumped out 15, 20 and 25% per year - far greater than what's typically available in today's stock market.

4. Tax advantages. In most places governments try to promote small business and entrepreneurship. They incentivize job creators through grants, tax credits and deductions. For example, I once worked with a real estate developer in New York City whose investors received major tax benefits for financing his projects. The buildings they developed provided clean, affordable rental suites to residents in dilapidated areas of town. The city rewarded companies like his for improving certain neighborhoods and spurring local employment. The investors profited not only from the real estate, but from the tax treatment as well. I've invested in similar opportunities in Arizona and Texas.

5. Flexibility. Unlike purchasing stocks or mutual funds, an investor has ample room to negotiate the terms of the deal. Little is set in stone with private investments. For example, he might ask for additional collateral, more equity, purchase options or buy-back clauses. If he doesn't get what he wants, he doesn't need to invest. I recently did a deal where I didn't allow the entrepreneur to earn a penny without returning 100% of my capital first, plus an additional 15%. Only after that point could he participate in the profits. This ability to negotiate is key to turning a good investment into a great one.

6. Social consequences. Businesses can create jobs, develop technology, increase living standards and make a tangible impact on the community. Some of the greatest human advances have been financed, facilitated or created by companies. For investors like myself who hold the virtues of business highly, this is an extremely important benefit of investing with entrepreneurs.

7. Access to more entrepreneurs. An offshoot of investing with an entrepreneur is that you will likely meet others in his network. This can open your portfolio to new, exciting and profitable ventures that you otherwise wouldn't have known about.

Questions to Ask Before Investing
With An Entrepreneur

1. Do I trust you on a personal level? There are a lot of sketchy people in the world, and some of them include entrepreneurs. Regardless of how attractive an investment opportunity seems, none of that matters if the entrepreneur is a thief, liar or crook. What does your gut tell you? If you have a bad feeling about someone's character, giving them your money may not be wise. Investing with someone scrupulous is a good first step to protecting your capital.

For example, in December 2014 I planned to purchase an investment property. The deal was simple: I'd put up the cash and the entrepreneur would do all of the hard work. He'd acquire the house, renovate it and find a tenant. Based on the numbers he presented it seemed like an amazing deal. Further into the due diligence process, though, I discovered that he inflated some of the figures to make it more appealing to investors. I pulled out immediately because I no longer trusted him. In my mind I thought, if he lied about the numbers, what else might he lie about? The irony was that the true figures were still highly attractive. I still would have invested if he was honest.

2. How have your other investors done? Experience is something that cannot be bought. If the entrepreneur has a strong, verifiable track record of providing other investors with outstanding returns - that's always a plus.

3. How is the deal structured? New investors beware. Understanding how and why an investment is structured is crucial. As I mentioned above, I've seen grand slam investments go sour because of flaws in the way they were assembled. As part of your due diligence, consider the following factors:

How will my portion of the investment be taxed?

When the investment produces returns, who gets paid first?

What share of the profits am I entitled to, and is it enough to make the investment worthwhile?

What legal entity is being used to facilitate the investment (e.g.: corporation, limited partnership, trust, joint venture agreement, etc.), and does it make sense?

Do you have any control of the asset or are you a silent partner?

What rules govern the investment agreement?

Do the investment agreement and deal structure protect your interests?

Each deal is different and it's important to know your investment inside-out. If you're new to the business, get help from people with experience. Regardless of what the investment is, I always have a lawyer go through the paperwork with a fine-toothed comb.

4. Can my investment be secured with collateral?
Are there assets available to secure your investment?
What can the entrepreneur offer? If there is collateral
available I strongly recommend hiring a lawyer to help
you with this. Don't rely on the entrepreneur's lawyer
- get your own. I saw an instance where the investor
believed the legal paperwork was sufficient to tie his
capital to a piece of real estate in case the deal went
sideways. He later on discovered that it wasn't. While
the deal hasn't gone awry, the investment is now far
riskier than what he originally intended.

5. How and when does the entrepreneur get paid?
Everyone has their own perspective on this. I usually
won't make an investment unless the entrepreneur
agrees to forgo any compensation until my capital is
returned. First, this compels the entrepreneur to work
as hard as possible to pay me back. Second, it ensures
that he can't dilute my investment by taking fees or
salaries, etc. Again, this is my personal preference and
you should do whatever makes the most sense for you.

6. Is the entrepreneur a professional? When I'm
working with an entrepreneur, I expect him to be a
professional. Last year, for example, I turned down
a potentially lucrative real estate deal because the
entrepreneur's unprofessionalism made me distrust
his abilities. This particular person preferred to type
out mortgage statements on his iPhone rather than
providing me with the actual documents during the
due diligence period. In my opinion, if the entrepreneur

isn't serious about being a professional, he won't take my money seriously either.

Investing With Entrepreneurs Sounds Complicated

And it is. Much more so than buying stocks or mutual funds. It involves a broad range of skills and expertise, and can be daunting for any beginner. However, there's one element that we haven't yet discussed which will make the process much simpler: you cannot make these investments alone.

In my view, few people are talented enough to thoroughly understand everything about business, law, real estate, accounting, deal structures, taxes, banking and investment potential. I'm sure not, and I don't know anyone who is. Instead of going it solo, you should align yourself with a team of partners who are experts in places where you aren't. Build relationships, refer business to each other and nurture your connections over time. Having a good team of experienced professionals to help you along your journey will save you from a lot of headaches, and a lot of money. If you've never done this before, don't be discouraged. Investing with entrepreneurs can be hard work – but believe me, the money is worth it.

How to Meet Entrepreneurs

The world is a very small place thanks to the internet. Entrepreneurs exist in communities everywhere (including yours); the trick is to find them. Below are ways to find entrepreneurs. And guess what: they all want you to invest with them! Here are a few ways to get started.

1. Use Google to search for terms like [your city] real estate investment club, etc.

2. Join your local chamber of commerce

3. Attend wealth seminars. They're a popular hangout for entrepreneurs

4. Look up local small business conventions

5. Connect with a friend on social media who's self-employed. You never know where the relationship will take you.

6. Join online communities. There are thousands out there.

7. Find people that you're inspired by and try to connect with them. Many successful entrepreneurs are public speakers and travel to cities across the world.

Now's Your Time to Begin

If you don't yet feel comfortable with investing with entrepreneurs, that's no problem. Start to build out your network and at least get exposure to the scene. Continuously educate yourself and work to increase your financial intelligence. Eventually you'll get there.

WHY I AVOID STOCKS
AND MUTUAL FUNDS LIKE
A NASTY DISEASE

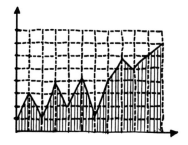

WHY I AVOID STOCKS AND MUTUAL FUNDS LIKE A NASTY DISEASE

If you invest in stocks and mutual funds, you're probably terrible at it. Seriously, the chances are that you're awful. I don't say that to be rude; it's just a fact. In an article published in Business Insider last year it was shown that between 1993 and 2013 the average investor underperformed just about every single asset class in the markets, except for a small portion of Asian equities. But when it came to energy, financials, health care, technology, consumer staples, corporate bonds, gold - you name it - investors around the world consistently made poor asset choices for 20 years.

In fact, cash even did better than the average investor. That's right. Boring, old dust-collecting cash is a more lucrative asset because the average person is just that bad at investing!

The truth is that for most people, stocks and mutual funds are poor investments. They exist on a platform that places retail investors like you and me at a major disadvantage, and it's almost impossible to do well year-over-year. Unless you're a high-frequency trading computer or you run a Wall Street hedge fund, you are most likely going to get creamed. And in doing so, you'll help a lot of people get rich along the way.

Therefore I avoid stocks and their ugly stepsister, mutual funds, like the plague. Let's get into why.

#1: You Have No Control in the Markets

I've written lots about how I made my money. If you've made it this far in the book, by now you know that I've been able to make investments that yield high returns with little risk because I maintain a lot of control over my assets. I'm able to understand what the risks are and then install safeguards to mitigate against them. Oftentimes, I can almost guarantee that my investment will be successful. That's what I love about investing with entrepreneurs. There's enough flexibility and room to negotiate to allow the investor the protection he wants.

The stock market, however, does not provide for that kind of risk management. While an investor can place stop orders and hedge bets with derivatives, the performance and direction of the markets is beyond anyone's control. Will stocks rise tomorrow or will they fall? Which sectors will do better than the others? Will turmoil in the Middle East send oil prices through the roof overnight? Where will the markets be in five years? Nobody knows - especially not the common investor. The stock market is a colossal playing field that is inherently unpredictable. Sometimes it ebbs and flows, and other times it crashes and soars.

Understanding the Markets

To understand why the markets are so capricious, it's important know what they are and how they work. From there, it becomes apparent why the average investor is at risk.

In short, the stock market is a place where public companies trade. Businesses list on exchanges (NYSE, TSX, NASDAQ, OTC, etc.) in order to raise capital, and in return for investors' money they offer shares in the company. That's done through an Initial Public Offering (IPO), and firms who've done that have "gone public."

Once a company goes public, investors can then buy and sell their shares with others. At this point, they're no longer buying shares from the company; rather they're trading them with other investors who now own stock. For example, if you were to invest in The Coca Cola Company today, you'd be buying shares from another investor and not from the company itself.

Why Do Stock Prices Rise and Fall?

Stock prices are a function of supply and demand. They rise and fall based on trading activity. For example, if Apple has more buyers than sellers at a particular moment, its price will increase. But, if investors start dumping their shares, the price will fall. Stock prices do not reflect a company's performance. Instead, they echo investors' actions.

The next question is then, why do investors buy and sell their stocks?

The answer, again, has little to do with company performance. Instead, investors trade based on their confidence in and predictions for a business. For example, if they believe Microsoft has a bright future because of increasing sales and a growing market for its products, they might buy shares in it anticipating a price increase. Conversely, if they feel that it is on a decline, they may sell Microsoft shares and reduce their exposure to it.

Note, however, the words *feel* and *believe*. Investors gather information about the economy, companies, markets and politics - usually through the news, financial statements and the internet - and base their decisions on what they know. But what happens if the information they receive is incorrect or not fully accurate? Or what if they react irrationally?

For example, in the summer of 2013 Canadian telecom giants Rogers and Telus were threatened by rumors of Verizon entering the market. Verizon, a behemoth American business, could potentially chomp into their profits and change the industry forever. Analysts cut their target prices, investors sold their shares and Rogers and Telus' price fell. To their delight, however, it was months later announced that the news about Verizon turned out to be false.

During that time of uncertainty, both Rogers and Telus

shed millions of dollars in value. Investors' fears were stoked and ambivalence dominated that sector of the market. But let's look at why exactly prices fell. Was it because Rogers and Telus reported poor financials? Were revenues falling or customers leaving? Were those businesses on a steep decline? No. Instead, investors speculated that those companies would suffer if Verizon was to enter Canada. They were spooked by rumors circulating in the media and on the web, and they dumped their shares.

Thus, stock prices rise and fall because of investors' sentiment and perception. Shares are bought when confidence is high and they're sold when it's low. Markets are a reflection of human emotion and attitude, not the realities of business.

Of course, the telecom case above is only one example. In fact, it's just the tip of the iceberg. In most cases, retail investors mistime and misunderstand the markets. They are simply unable to act rationally. It has been well documented that the majority of investors buy when prices are high and sell when they're low - which is exactly the opposite of what should be done.

Rather than investing in a market dominated by sentimental investors and skewed asset prices, I prefer to invest where businesses can't be swung so easily. Earning profits is a financial, not emotional, game. The more variables that can be eliminated the greater the chances of success. Thus, I place my capital in ventures that can largely be controlled.

#2: Retail Investors are Ill-Equipped for the Stock Market

Unfortunately, sentimental and emotionally unstable humans are only one problem with the stock market. Most investments are actually made by massive hedge funds, pension funds, financial institutions and high-frequency trading computers which exploit minute arbitrages in prices.

Against Goliath-sized companies with billions of dollars in capital, retail investors do not stand a chance. These firms can plow exorbitant sums of money and prop up prices, or they can sell stock and cause markets to tank. They're equipped with faster trading systems and sophisticated algorithms that can snatch the best deals before the common investor is made aware of them. Importantly, they're often privy to information before it reaches the media.

Mom-and-pop investors are slower, less-informed, more emotional (than trading computers) and have only a fraction of the buying power that these companies do. Their capital is truly at the mercy of market movers and trading giants. It's a tough business for anyone to do well in.

No Country for Old (and Experienced) Men

Of course, one could always learn to be a better stock trader, right? If you take the time to practice, get informed and learn to ride the markets couldn't you do quite well?

While that might make intuitive sense, the facts suggest otherwise. Research shows that even industry professionals rarely do well in the markets. To be precise, they are awful at picking stocks. Only 22% of financial advisors' recommendations can keep up with the market index; the other 78% underperform it. That means that if the stock market goes up in a year, an advisor's portfolio most likely went up by less (if at all). If the market declines, an advisor's portfolio probably fell even further.

4 out of 5 financial advisers would do better for their clients if they invested their money in a low-cost unmanaged exchange-traded fund (ETF) that simply replicates the stock market. The less involved humans are, the better the chances are for success. In fact, even billionaire investor Warren Buffett doesn't trust professionals to pick stocks. Rather than having professional money managers invest his assets after he passes, he willed his estate to be left in ETFs.

If the industry's best and brightest can't do well in the markets, it's nearly impossible for the average investor to do so either. Knowing that I could never compete with institutions and trading companies, I bowed out of the market a long time ago.

#3: Sloppy-Second Returns

Have you ever noticed that when companies go public, it's always the initial investors who become overnight millionaires? You never hear about the average Joe going from zero to hero after buying into an IPO. For example, when Facebook went public in 2012, founder Mark Zuckerberg made $1.15 billion in a matter of hours. It's always the primary investors, the ones who got in before the public offering, who make a killing. Why is that?

The fact is that much of a company's value has already been realized by the time it lists on a stock market. For an investor, there's very little upside in comparison to when it was privately-held. If you look at the lifespan of a business, there is exponentially more money to be made if you invest at the ground level than there is once it's already a multi-million dollar operation. By the time a company is large enough to go public on a major stock exchange, the initial shareholders have reaped much of the rewards. Once they sell their shares to investors in an IPO, they laugh all the way to the bank.

Thus, a post-IPO investor might make 10% per year on a stock. But the founders and initial shareholders often make upwards of 10,000% in the public offering. Which would you rather receive? As a venture capital guy, I'm inherently opposed to being a secondary investor. Instead, I prefer to be on the other side of the table. I invest early and would rather sell my shares to the public, and not the other way around.

Bad Arguments for Investing in Stocks

Given that most retail investors have high exposure to the stock market, it's understandable why some wouldn't want to hear the reasons against it. Below are commonly-used but ultimately straw man arguments for investing there.

Bad Argument #1: Warren Buffett Does It

As mentioned earlier in this book, a classic rebuttal is, "Well, what about Warren Buffett? He made billions by trading stocks." The logic behind this argument is that Warren Buffett is only human and therefore can be matched or even outdone. He gives hope to the average stock investor.

While it's true that Warren Buffett is a great stock investor, he didn't actually make his money by picking stocks. It's a common misunderstanding that he put a few thousand bucks in the markets and later turned it into billions. Instead, Buffett got rich by raising capital from investors.

Bad Argument #2: the Stock Market Always Goes Up Over Time

Another routine (and incorrect) comment about the stock market is that it will always rise over time. Industry professionals laud the inevitable long-term growth of the markets as though it's a theorem. In the same way that we know an apple hits the earth after falling from a tree because of gravity, they know that markets always go up eventually. That's why financial advisors tell their clients to invest for the long term.

Unfortunately, people who buy into that theory are confusing past performance with a prediction of future results. The stock market did certainly always rise in the 20th century. In fact, if you invested $1,000 in 1900 you would have turned it into nearly $20 million by 1999. However, that century also experienced the greatest economic expansion in human history. During that time, enormous multinational companies were built, transportation and trade were made more efficient, wages grew and trillions of dollars in wealth were created. The internet was born, nuclear energy was discovered, the airplane was invented, the first robot was assembled and the hit single Ice Ice Baby was released. Gene splicing, cell phones, the word processor, credit cards, the solar cell, optic fiber and the microchip all transformed civilization. It was an era of unprecedented prosperity. With that kind of growth of course investors would be confident and cause the markets to rise.

Today, however, is a very different age. Thanks to rampant financial mismanagement the world suffered an economic meltdown in 2008. Since then, jobs have become scarcer, wages are stagnant, Europe's economy flounders and America's no longer steams as fervently as it once did. Businesses are cautious about investment and often hoard cash for a rainy day instead of investing it. Gone are the times of large corporate pensions because companies can no longer afford them. And most importantly, the largest-ever generation of humans is beginning to exit the workforce, only to be replaced by millions of young adults who are unable to find quality employment.

It's understandable that someone back in the 1990s would think that the stock market always rises in the long term. After all, two generations had seen little to suggest otherwise. But after 2008, when investors are unsure of what the future holds, it is ludicrous to simply assume (and tell clients) that the stock market will always go up. With a lackluster economy, high unemployment and underemployment and changing demographics, investors are not as confident as they once were. Nobody can predict with certainty where the markets will be in the long term.

Mutual Funds are the Worst of all Worlds

You may be wondering why I've lumped in mutual funds with stocks in this chapter. They are different investments, so why am I discussing them here?

In fact, stocks and mutual funds are closely related. A mutual fund is simply an investment fund that owns a basket of stocks, bonds and even other mutual funds. They typically hold 50 to 150 different investments. I relate them to putting rotten fruit in a bucket. The rotten fruit are the stocks and the mutual fund is the bucket. Yum.

Mutual funds were created to ~~make money for banks~~ provide investors with a diverse, professionally managed portfolio of assets to help them limit their risk and maximize returns. Unfortunately, they do nothing of the sort. Instead, they possess all of the downsides associated with stocks, plus more. They add several layers of management and administration fees, which substantially dilute investors' profits. Unsurprisingly, mutual funds have done a huge disservice to investors. In 2014 it was revealed that the average mutual fund investor received an embarrassing 1.9% annual return over the past 30 years.

Conclusion

I think I've made it pretty clear that I'm not a big supporter of either stocks or mutual funds. To me, they're poor investments designed for unsophisticated investors. With that said, it's my opinion that if you're unwilling to take the time to become a sophisticated investor, then they are a viable vehicle to build wealth with. You won't make much money with them, but they're probably better than blowing your cash.

One of the greatest issues that I take with stocks and mutual funds is that salespeople, administrators and institutions make a lot of money offering a product that most likely won't do well for the client. Moreover, it's not as though these investments make up a small portion of people's portfolios; these are the primary assets that clients own.

Of course, people already know that most financial services companies are self-serving. It's common knowledge that many put their interests ahead of their clients'. The most obvious example is banks who in 2008 purposely sold their clients toxic investments and then bet against them. These kinds of scandals are so common in finance that people hardly bat an eye today.

The bigger question is, why do people keep going back to them?

How is it that mutual funds can earn 1.9% per year for 30 years and still be clients' number-one investment choice? Why do people hire financial advisors for investments when they're statistically proven to be useless? Why do investors keep buying stocks when they rarely make money with them? Financial services is the only industry where you can repeatedly underperform for your clients and still earn their business each year. Why is it like this?

The answer boils down to the widespread lack of financial education in today's world. Since most people have no knowledge of how to make investments, the void is filled by the commission-heavy, results-light financial services industry. Large companies in the business dominate all aspects of finance to the point that people don't even know that there are alternatives to stocks, bonds and mutual funds.

Of course, one can only place the blame on banks and Wall Street tycoons for so long. At some point, investors also need to wake up. If you keep losing money - or if you never seem to make money consistently - you are doing something wrong. Something needs to change. The solution doesn't lie in the hot new investment that your broker calls you about. It's in you. How much time are you willing to invest in your financial education? How hard are you going to work? I speak from experience when I say that a lot of money can be made if you take the time to learn how. If you aren't ready to make the effort, though, don't expect your wealth to increase either.

INVESTING FOR
EARLY RETIREMENT

INVESTING FOR EARLY RETIREMENT

I believe that investing in a retirement account is among the most prudent steps a person can take towards financial security. Most in the west aren't able to save or invest an adequate amount. The bulk of their wealth is held in their homes and they are generally "cash poor," meaning that they don't have enough disposable income. By regularly contributing to an RRSP (Canada), Roth IRA (USA), Superannuation (Australia) or other retirement schemes they can gradually build a nest egg on which they can rely in their golden years. Moreover, governments typically offer tax breaks to further incentivize contributions.

In my case, however, I don't use a retirement account. While I think they're invaluable to the average investor, to me they serve no purpose. I instead prefer to hold most of my assets elsewhere.

Retirement Should Be a Triangle, Not a Diamond

The first reason for why I reject using an RRSP is a philosophical one. I'm inherently opposed to its structure. In general, retirement accounts function as follows: a person contributes cash into it and may receive a tax reward for doing so, typically in the form of a credit or a deduction. Once her cash is in the account, she can then choose to invest it and will be exempt from paying taxes earned on her capital. If she invests early enough she could therefore potentially earn decades of tax-free growth.

Upon retirement she can then withdraw cash from the account, and at that point will pay taxes on the income she receives from it. However, since she'll be in her 60s or 70s, her lifestyle expenses will likely be lower and will thus be taxed less. By the time she passes away she'll have little left in her retirement account because it served its purpose of sustaining her for years after she retired.

The issue that I take with this system is that the retirement account takes a diamond shape. It is smallest when you're young because you haven't contributed much to it. By the time you retire, however, it should be at its greatest value because you've made decades worth of contributions and investments in it. During retirement, since you draw from it regularly to support your post-career lifestyle, it then begins to shrink. As you grow older your retirement assets continue to diminish. When you die, there will likely be next to nothing left in it.

Retirement accounts presuppose that people will downsize when they stop working. They assume that after 40 years in the workforce a person is happy to reduce their quality of life and cut down expenses. They'll have paid off their mortgage, their children will have moved out and they will need less money. That supposition simply doesn't describe my goals for the future.

Instead, as you already know, my investment strategy is to buy assets that pay income monthly. If I earn $10,000 per month from my investments but only need $9,000 to live on, I can then reinvest that extra $1,000 and continue to add to my portfolio. As such, I become wealthier each month and should theoretically be at my richest when I'm on my deathbed. I should have been at my poorest at 23 and will hopefully be at my wealthiest at 103.

Moreover, I also disapprove of the notion of working hard for 40 years only to retire to a minimalistic lifestyle. To the contrary, in my post-business years I hope I'll spend more money than I ever could because I'd have more time on my hands! I would vacation for long periods at beautiful resorts, buy a bigger house for when my children and grandchildren visit, purchase more cars and dine out more frequently. I might even do some philanthropy, pay for my grandchildren's education or give more to charity. But regardless of what I choose to do with my wealth, I most certainly object to limiting my quality of life after spending decades to create it. For that reason, alone, retirement accounts don't work for me.

My Preferred Investments Aren't
Retirement Account-Eligible

The second reason for rejecting retirement accounts is because the investments I make can't usually be held within them. Rather, stocks, mutual funds, bonds, publicly-traded entities and some limited partnerships are typically the only RRSP-eligible assets. I would not be able to, for example, buy a commercial building using retirement funds or loan money to an entrepreneur. Because of how limited retirement accounts are I don't use them.

Instead, I prefer to hold the bulk of my assets within corporations. This structure allows me to pay less in taxes while also providing legal protection should one of my deals ever be sued. As well, they offer a high degree of privacy that renders it difficult for the government, banks, lawyers, competitors or anyone else to discover what I own. Done correctly, corporations can be opaque and its shareholders and beneficial owners can be nearly untraceable.

Thus, my corporations are effectively my retirement plan. They earn income on a daily basis which I can use to finance my lifestyle. Their assets grow monthly because I reinvest any income I don't spend. And unlike an RRSP or other vehicles, I have the freedom to make any investments that I choose. While I miss out from tax-exempt growth and certain deductions that retirement accounts provide, using a corporation makes the most financial sense for me.

In my opinion, if your objective is similar to what mine was then a retirement account may not be the right fit. If your intent is to buy private, passive revenue-producing assets and retire on that income then you might have to look at another solution. Whatever you do, though, don't blindly set up a retirement account without understanding the implications of doing so. Correctly structuring your portfolio is paramount to financial freedom.

HOW TO MAKE $100,000 WITHOUT PUTTING UP A PENNY

HOW TO MAKE $100,000 WITHOUT PUTTING UP A PENNY

The greatest challenge that I faced when I first set out to build wealth was my lack of capital. At 23, I had no savings, no assets, a low income and debts that I needed to repay. Without capital to work with I thought it impossible to take meaningful steps towards becoming rich. It seemed like the classic chicken and egg scenario: you can't make money without having money to begin with. How do you make investments and build wealth if you have no capital to invest? It's a catch-22.

Of course, before long I learned that the old adage, "it takes money to make money," simply wasn't true. It's a misconception. As I mention elsewhere in this book, having cash helps but it isn't the only resource available to acquire assets. It's also neither the safest nor the most profitable tool to use. Assets are, well, an asset - but they're not a prerequisite to getting rich.

Instead, it's what's inside your head (and how you use it) that ultimately makes you wealthy. The extent of your financial knowledge and the investment you're willing to make in it is key. What and who you know are far more important than what's accumulated in your bank account.

In this chapter I'm going to show you that it's entirely possible to invest and earn hundreds of thousands of dollars without having any capital to start with. In it, I'm going to walk you through a real-life example of an investment I'm currently making. After all is said and done, I will likely exit the deal with a $100,000 profit. And best of all, it will have cost me nothing.

The Opportunity

At the time of writing I'm weeks away from acquiring a new piece of real estate. It's a two bedroom, one bath condominium not too far away from Vancouver. The condo is located in a small but rapidly-growing town that's also water-locked. The town borders the Pacific Ocean so there's only limited room for it to expand. If the population continues to grow, demand for residential real estate would likely increase along with prices. It's by all accounts a fundamentally great place to invest.

How I found the property is an unglamorous story. After casually browsing online I came across one that seemed oddly undervalued. It was part of a small residential building with ten condominiums, each selling for about $250,000. Comparable properties were going for $300,000 so it obviously caught my attention. Right away I wondered how they could be so cheap. Was there a pricing error on the website? The condos looked in pictures brand-new; what could be wrong with them?

The next morning I called the listing realtor. After a long conversation with him, followed by reading local news stories and blogs, I discovered why the properties were priced that way. They were, in fact, new and never before lived in and no renovations or upgrades would be needed. Instead, however, the problems lay in the building's history.

Seven years ago, in 2008, a developer had purchased the land to construct a 10-unit condominium complex on it. Only months after the project began, though, the subprime mortgage collapse occurred. The bank that provided the mortgage, like many others around the world, was crunched for credit and recalled the loan to the developer. Unable to come up with funds elsewhere, the firm defaulted on its obligations and the partially-complete building was seized by the bank.

In 2010 a second developer took over the property and completed its construction. All ten units and common areas were finished and ready to sell. However, this developer mistimed the project and apparently took it on too soon. Only 18 months after the Great Recession, the local real estate market had yet to recover and the appetite for new constructions was small. With poor financing conditions and little movement on the condos, the second developer also defaulted on its mortgage obligations and lost the property to the bank.

Having now foreclosed two times on the same building, the bank opted to wash its hands of it. The property was sold at a steep loss to a private equity firm, which currently owns it today.

The private equity firm, which had acquired the building for 30% of its value, immediately listed the condos on the market. This time, however, they could be priced so inexpensively that investors would find them irresistible. The firm also offered seller financing, meaning that buyers could acquire the condominiums with no down payment. Instead, monthly instalments of $1,000 could be made until it was paid off in full.

After researching similar properties, I learned that the average cost of rent in the area was about $1,300. This, of course, was $300 more than the required monthly instalments. It dawned on me that if I acquired the property and immediately rented it to a tenant, I would never need to fork over my own money for it. Instead, the tenant's rent payments would cover the $1,000 instalments and even generate a bit of extra income.

Today, I am weeks away from owning one of the condominium. Thanks to the local economy it's also in an area that's heavily demanded by renters, so finding one will doubtfully be a challenge. Soon I will have acquired a $250,000 piece of real estate without even making a down payment. Each month, my tenant's rent will pay off the financing and ultimately increase my wealth by about $10,000 per year.

If all goes to plan, after five years I will have built up about $50,000 in equity in the condominium. At that point, my plan is to sell it. Assuming market prices remain flat, I'll make $100,000 on the sale: half from the equity that the tenant built and half due to the fact that it's worth $50,000 more than I what I'm buying for. If I'm lucky, prices will increase and I can make even more.

Master Your Craft to Profit

People often say that real estate investing involves a lot of luck. It's about being in the right place at the right time, or knowing the right people. For instance, what are the chances that I would have found a building that had been foreclosed on twice and sold off at a 70% discount?

Of course, there is a degree of good fortune involved with any investment. There are some things, like sudden price drops or market swings, that nobody can predict. However, good real estate investors don't need to rely on luck; they can create their own. The truth is that there are always great real estate deals available. In every market in each city there are mispriced properties that can be profited from.

Real estate is an interesting asset because it comes with a lot of human baggage. For most people, it's the biggest purchase they'll ever make. Real estate involves families, history and often a lot of emotion. As such, the pricing can be irrational and ripe for investment opportunity.

Ultra-low prices often occur because of a "motivated seller." This is someone who needs to sell because of life circumstances. For example, if a person has to move to a new country for work in a month he might be desperate to sell his house before he leaves. Closing on real estate can take weeks so he would need to lock in a buyer as quickly as possible. To attract interest, he lists it on the market for well below its fair value. For investors, deals like this are prime.

Whatever the story, though, there are great buying opportunities everywhere. The trick is to be able to find them. That skill can separate amazing investments from average ones - and that's how you can make your millions.

To find the best deals you need to master the craft. You should know everything there is about your business and profit from your expertise. A great example is one of my associates, Paul. After losing his job as a tradesman he decided to make his living as a real estate investor in Grande Prairie, a small town in Alberta. He focussed on a niche property market of trailer homes rented by low-income families.

Over the course of months Paul dedicated himself to mastering his market. He learned about the local economy, what drives it and what might cause property prices there to fluctuate. He kept his fingers on the pulse of minimum-wage job growth, knowing that it would impact the demand for trailer homes. He learned to understand the real estate, how it's priced and what it can rent for. He also built relationships with every mortgage broker, realtor and lawyer involved in the niche industry.

Today, Paul is a guru in his own right. There's not an offer in his market that he isn't familiar with. He knows who is buying and selling, the quantity of local inventory and whether or not there's an opportunity for investment. As such, Paul has attracted a ton of capital from people who want to profit from the trailer home business. He now makes incredible money by raising capital from investors to buy and flip trailers and taking a cut of the profits.

Conclusion

Paul is a perfect example of someone who used his brain and not money to make investments. Today he owns a portfolio of dozens of properties, all of which were acquired with other people's funds. While some might call it "lucky" to find deeply discounted real estate, that's a very short-sighted perspective. Great opportunities are usually found by people like Paul: professionals who have mastered a craft and know where to look for them.

If you can become an expert in a certain field and help others profit from your knowledge, there's a world of fortune to be made. This same concept applies to any industry; not just real estate. To make your money like Paul did, take something you're good at and become great at it. Be better than everyone else and let the world know that you're the industry authority. If you can truly master your craft, promote yourself well and show others that you can make them money – you'll surely do well.

Of course, sometimes earning large profits with no money down doesn't even require expertise. In the case of my condo investment, it simply meant keeping my eyes open and understanding enough about the project to know that there's an opportunity to profit. Regardless, don't limit yourself by believing that you can only get rich if you have capital to invest. Money is a resource, but it's not the only one at your disposal.

ON ATTITUDE AND BEHAVIOUR

ON ATTITUDE AND BEHAVIOUR

I've peppered this book with words like "often," "usually," "typically" and "frequently" because business and investing can never be a sure thing. There are no guarantees in the game and we all run the risk of absolute failure. One comment that I can make without hesitancy, though, is that your plight towards financial freedom will not be easy. You'll face any number of obstacles, including failed partnerships, delays, mistimed investments, poor tax planning and cost overruns. Depending on your journey you may even face government scrutiny and lawsuits.

However, it's without question that the greatest challenge you'll face is the emotional taxation of being an entrepreneur or an investor. The waters that you'll wade are by definition uncharted and the stress of the unknown can be soul-crushing. Many of your nights will be spent wondering why your venture isn't progressing the way that you thought it would. You'll doubt yourself and lose not only your confidence, but also the confidence of others. You'll question the hair-pullingly long hours you spend troubleshooting your roadblocks and wonder whether it's all worth it. Why do I work so hard and for so long on something that never produces any results? Why can't my enterprise, an expression of my pride, ideas, thoughts and money, ever seem to progress?

The discouragement, stagnation and emotional ups and downs that you, I and everyone like us will face are the ultimate catalyst for failure. Most entrepreneurs and investors cannot stomach months and years of disappointment, uncertainty, risk and little financial return. The anxiety can be overpowering. Thus, they bounce around from idea to idea, only to find that the next venture is no easier than the last. Eventually they quit and abandon all hopes of wealth, assets and financial independence.

With that said, it's imperative that you know this in advance. Building your wealth is a business of emotional maturity more than it is intellectualism, labour or anything else. An ingenious idea will forever remain a thought if you don't have the wherewithal to conquer, compartmentalize and harness your sentiments.

In this chapter I'll share my method for maintaining emotional durability, which hinges upon the principle of acceptance. While my strategy is personal in that I only know it works for me, I'd be remiss if I didn't shed light on what I do. Glean what you can from the paragraphs below and adapt it to yourself accordingly.

Acceptance

There are several truths in business that are simply inescapable. They're like gravity; always there and impossible to remove. As the Borg once said in Star Trek, resistance is futile. Attempting to fight them is an exhausting emotional exercise and one that assures eventual failure. Rather than trying to circumvent or overpower the following three laws, I've chosen to accept them instead. I understand that they will always exist and I try to incorporate them into my ventures' strategies.

Truth #1: Lag

The first truth is that it will take time before you'll see the fruits of your labor. In spite of how much effort you put into a venture you likely won't realize results in the short or even medium term. If you are investing capital you will need to wait before you have enough to impact your portfolio's growth. If you are building a business, it can take years before your clients like and trust you enough to give you their money. Establishing your company as legitimate, knowledgeable, credible and authoritative requires time in the market. This concept of lag is universal but still unknown amongst beginners who hope to see immediate results. Ignorance about it floors entrepreneurs who expect their hard work to pay off quickly.

A good example of lag is my own website, AlexisAssadi. net, which I launched in 2013 to write publicly about my experiences. Building a large, responsive and loyal readership was my goal, so I wrote weekly articles which catered to the interests of my target demographic.

After a year of writing dozens of lengthy pieces my online presence was still only a pittance. I averaged about 300 viewers per month and was practically invisible on the internet. I was disappointed but enjoyed writing nonetheless and continued to create content.

By the summer of 2014 my monthly audience had grown to about 1,000. In addition to writing consistently, I had also spent money on plugins, platforms and other gadgets to improve my site. I learned about HTML coding, search engine optimization, content marketing and I studied everything I could about the online business model. The results from my efforts were still low, but my site was at least progressing. I could handle working hard on it because I could see light at the tunnel's end.

Unfortunately, though, just as my readership began to expand AlexisAssadi.net was hacked. Someone or something had breached my security and planted spammy pages with links to an obscure French website. I was quickly blackballed by search engines and in October my presence on Google plummeted. I was lucky to have three people a day visit.

The frustration that I felt at the time was unbearable. While my site was never intended to be a major money maker, it was my personal goal to see it succeed. I wanted to establish myself as an authoritative voice on investing and help break the mould of personal finance. The website had become my baby. To have spent thousands of hours and constantly lose money, only to get hacked and lose my readers, was a serious blow to my spirit. After 18 months, no real results and now a site hack, I wanted to throw in the towel.

This chapter is not about my website so I'll shorten the story here. By mid-2015 AlexisAssadi.net received thousands of monthly viewers and plenty of positive feedback. It also became an income-producing asset that requires only passive management. In fact, the chances are that you purchased this book through the site! While it's no Investopedia or Wall Street Journal, AlexisAssadi.net is something that I'm proud of. It's a venture that I worked hard on and grows almost daily. The cherry on top is that it also provides a platform upon which I can use to increase my wealth.

Now, if you wonder whether I found a secret to catapult my readership after getting hacked, the answer is a disappointing "no." The only tool in my arsenal was stubborn consistency. Rather than giving up every time the tide turned against my site, I spent two years learning, experimenting, testing and writing. I gradually built an audience by trying to give them value. Simply put, my "secret to success" was old-fashioned hard work over a long period of time. The lag between AlexisAssadi.net's launch and eventual growth was more than two years.

The above example is par for the course in business. Whether it took search engines a long time to like my content or my early material wasn't strong enough for readers to return frequently, I'll probably never know. But the fact is that there will always be a time lag between when you put in effort and when you see results.

Most people become discouraged when they don't receive short-term gratification. Instead, they should understand lag and plan for it. Expect at least a twelve month delay for any initiative to produce results. Rather than feeling frustrated or confused, use that time to build up other elements of your venture.

Truth #2: Uncertainty

Business is an inherently unpredictable animal. It's impossible to accurately understand the future or to guess which obstacles lie ahead. While you can certainly manage risk there are some things that just come out of nowhere. Total control does not exist. This second truth conflicts with people's natural desire for a degree of certainty before rolling out a new venture. The greater the investment, the deeper the anxiety and the harder it is to remain calm under pressure.

For instance, I got involved with a venture last year which we believed (and still do) will revolutionize a major industry in Canada (note: it's a sensitive subject so I need to speak about it vaguely here). It's an incredible product assembled by one of the most impressive businesspeople I've come across and it could literally benefit millions of Canadians. It seemed like a home run.

Shortly after launching, though, our program was unexpectedly shut down by a government agency. Its officials believed that we were violating provincial laws and immediately halted our activities. As you might imagine, the sudden pounce on us was disturbing to say the least. It felt like running a 100-yard sprint and hitting a wall after five metres.

After a six-week investigation, though, we were eventually cleared of any wrongdoing. We thus went about our business and continued to grow. In some ways we were glad that this happened so early because we could get the government out of our way before we got big. It was also a confidence boost to know that our program was impenetrable by their lawyers.

A few months later, however, we again received notice that we were being investigated; this time by another regulator. This agency supervises the same industry as the previous one but has jurisdiction over a different province in Canada. While we weren't suspended, it threw a major wrench at our expansion plans by adding a healthy dose of, "what the hell happens if they shut us down?" At the time of writing we're working with the regulator and expect the same result as before.

Until then, however, there's plenty of uncertainty surrounding our business. We know from prior dealings with different regulators that the government doesn't always have to obey the law. It can change or ignore the rules because it has limitless resources and limited accountability. To disagree with them requires extremely deep pockets. As such, there's a very real possibility that the hundreds of thousands of dollars we invested in this venture could all go to waste.

The stark reality is that this kind of uncertainty comes with the territory. We know that all of our efforts may very well have been in futility. We could be shut down, fined or sanctioned and could walk away with a failed company. As with lag, I know that tumult is a simple fact in the business world and choose not to stress about it. While I'm confident we'll succeed I know how disappointed I'll be if we fail. But rather than worry, I accept the reality and don't bog myself down in negativity.

Truth #3: Hard Work and Consistency Always Prevail

The third truth about business is that becoming successful requires a lot of hard work. It means late nights, early mornings and plenty of sacrifices. It requires unbridled dedication that few can sustain for very long.

Of course, anyone can work hard when they feel the adrenaline of passion pumping through their veins. It's easy to plow forward when the wind is at your back. However, the real test of one's mettle comes when times are tough. Can an entrepreneur work hard when she not only doubts herself, but when everyone else doubts her, too? Can she push beyond a constant stream of failures and disappointments?

Most people can endure a beating for a short period of time. They can deal with weeks or even months of setbacks. Everyone has a breaking point, though, and will eventually recoil. The mark of someone destined for success is a person who can stick it out for the long term. Can they last in the ring and take on blow after blow until they finally reach their goal?

One of the best examples I've come across is a friend of mine, who I'll refer to as James to protect his privacy. In the course of a decade his company rose, fell and rose again in one of the most impressive bouts of persistence I've seen.

James' business, which again I prefer to leave confidential, started from humble beginnings. After five years, though, it grew from just a few employees to hundreds of staff across America. It was a rapidly-moving firm with seemingly endless potential.

After reaching a peak in 2007, however, the business encountered several simultaneous disasters; first and foremost was a declining economy. A result of the sub-prime mortgage crisis, the niche in which James operated had withered from tens of thousands of potential customers in the US to less than 8,000. With a weakened financial position and poor revenue projections, a $10 million line of credit that had been extended to James' company was recalled by two lenders.

The sudden withdrawal of the loan came at the worst possible time. James had already used up $8 million and with a lower volume of sales he intended to dip into the remaining $2 million to cover his short-term costs. A recall would mean that he'd not only default on his upcoming payments, but that he'd need to repay $8 million immediately.

However, the debt burden was only part of James' problems. To reduce expenses he would now need to lay off employees, many of whom had been loyal to him for years. They were like family and several had even relocated their spouses and children for the company. James' staff would lose their jobs and, given the economy, would likely be unable to find something as well-paying. To add salt to their wounds, he had insufficient funds to offer them a respectable severance package.

From there began an eight-year struggle for James to keep his business afloat. He raised private capital to replace his line of credit, but to attract it during an economic upheaval required giving investors exorbitant interest rates. While the immediate need for $8 million was gone, his company was now encumbered by massive debt costs each month. As well, he had fallen behind on payments he owed to contractors, accountants and telecom providers and was now being hassled by collection agencies.

Since 2007 I have watched James and his company fight through a dozen setbacks that all occurred as a chain reaction to the loan recall. Each obstacle looked as though they'd be the straw that broke the camel's back. From financing rejections to lawsuits and debt collectors, his business has seen it all. Every time, however, James managed to gather the resources he needed to push forward.

In 2015, his company finally returned to profit. While the numbers were still thin and he had a fraction of his former staff, it was nonetheless an important milestone. He no longer ran the danger of closing down shop. At the time of writing, James' business is again growing and has shed many of the problems that pinned it down for eight years.

James is living proof that indefatigable hard work and consistency are a mandatory ingredient in the recipe to success. He spent years untangling a business on the brink of insolvency and brought it back to life. Few others could bear the eight-year daily stresses of going bankrupt and losing it all.

Incessant hard work is a truth that must be accepted, but it can also be taken comfort in. It helps to know that every other successful businessperson has gone through a similar struggle. As such, each time one of my ventures takes a whipping, instead of walking away I remind myself that it's just part of the process. "Quitters never get rich" is a phrase that I repeat in my head constantly.

Conclusion

Business and investing are complex emotional experiences. While many say that there should be no emotion in business, it's difficult to work towards something that you aren't passionate about. Thus, there needs to be a healthy balance. In my opinion, learning to manage your feelings and not letting the negative ones impede your progress is a golden key to financial freedom. The easiest way to do this is to accept certain truths about the future of your business and incorporate them into your strategies. There is nothing more damaging than the paralysis caused by uncertainty or the fear of disappointment. Emotional intelligence will guide you through the peaks and valleys. Without it, you will surely quit before your venture has a fair chance of attaining success.

TAX MANAGEMENT

TAX MANAGEMENT

An essential part of investing is to both understand and manage the implications of taxation. A mistake that I made in my early days was to think that tax planning is only for wealthy individuals. As such, I rarely paid it attention and thus hampered my much-needed ROIs. I'd often inefficiently invest in assets that would yield attractive returns, only to give back 30% of what I gained to the government.

The reality is that in most places investors of all income levels will be impacted by taxes. They're a necessary evil that one needs to incorporate into her wealth-building strategy. While I don't advocate illegally dodging taxes, a prudent investor will seek to defer or minimize them. Since each country has its own laws there's no "one size fits all" method. Therefore, in this chapter I'll identify several broad factors I think you should consider before making an investment.

Before I do, though, I should mention this: basic tax planning does not require high-priced accountants and expensive licensed professionals. "I can't afford to learn about taxes" is not a legitimate excuse! In the age of the internet all of this information is available online. A simple Google search will help you find your jurisdiction's tax policies. While accountants are certainly helpful (and recommended), if you don't have one yet you shouldn't simply ignore your tax strategy.

Below are seven areas of taxation to understand before placing your capital into an asset.

Dividends, Interest Income, Capital Gains and Returns of Capital

In general, investment earnings will fall under four categories: dividends, interest, capital gains and returns of capital. Each classification is taxed differently. For example, in Canada income from interest is usually the least favorable. Conversely, a return of capital is tax-free. If and when your investment yields a return, how will it be taxed?

Investing Personally vs. Corporately

A corporation is a separate legal entity from an individual and therefore is taxed differently. In some cases they can be highly efficient. In 2010, for example, General Electric caused an uproar when it was discovered that it paid little income tax on over $5 billion in profits.

If you owned your investments through a company rather than personally, how would your taxation change? Are there some investments that would fare better corporately? If your tax burden lessened by doing so, would it be offset by the banking, accounting and filing costs of owning a company?

Passive Income vs. Active Income

Some jurisdictions offer better tax treatment to "active income" assets – ones which are actively managed as part of a business – than to passive income investments. Consider which class your investment falls under.

Business Structure

When investing in a non-personal entity (a company, for example), consider its legal structure. Is it a corporation, sole proprietorship, limited partnership, general partnership, trust or otherwise? Each entity receives different tax treatments under different circumstances.

Tax Flows

If you're investing into an asset that's highly tax-efficient, that doesn't necessarily mean that those advantages will be passed on to you. For example, you could invest in a company that pays little to no taxes, but you as the investor may still be liable for them. Consider how the tax burden flows between you and your asset.

International Taxation

If you are investing into a cross-border or overseas asset, consider the tax implications of doing so. In some cases your capital could be taxed in your home country as well as in the nation you're investing. Other times, however, countries have tax and trade agreements that nullify one of the respective levies.

Tax-Advantaged Accounts

Most countries offer tax-advantaged accounts to incentivize people to make investments. In Canada, for example, RRSPs and TFSAs are widely used. Consider whether your asset can or should be purchased through a tax-advantaged account.

Tax-Advantaged Investments

Countries frequently encourage investment into certain sectors of the economy. In some US states, for example, tax incentives are given to real estate developers who build clean and affordable apartment housing. In Canada, the government has historically encouraged investment into the mining, oil drilling and exploration businesses. Consider whether your asset is privy to similar incentives.

Conclusion

Tax management is a necessary part of investing. While I find it mind-numbing and boring, spending a few hours each year on my taxes is worth avoiding the frustration of losing out on returns. Personally, I use a range of both legal and ethical methods of reducing and deferring my tax liabilities. I hold some assets personally and others corporately, and I never invest in anything that could be taxed deeply enough to materially impact my net gains.

With that said, in a post-2008 world there is plenty of discussion surrounding the ethicality of tax reduction strategies. A growing number of people believe that taxes should be raised to counter bloated sovereign debts and add funding to government social programs. Businesses and wealthy individuals are often scolded, as General Electric was, for minimizing their own liabilities.

However, in my opinion the issue should not be about raising or lowering tax rates. Instead, it should be about how the money is spent. In both Canada and the US, local and federal governments are famous for being cost-inefficient. They're often cluttered by bureaucratic red tape, staffed with too many non-vital employees and frequently overspend taxpayers' dollars. In my view, the day I try to pay more in taxes is the day that the government uses my hard-earned dollars more wisely. Until then, I'd rather keep more of my money and invest it in businesses that add value to the economy.

HOW TO LOSE MONEY IN REAL ESTATE

HOW TO LOSE MONEY IN REAL ESTATE

Real property is the classic vehicle for wealth creation. It's coveted by investors of all experience levels as one of the best ways to earn a return on capital. If you look at the richest people in the world you'll find that a disproportionate number of them are real estate moguls.

Unfortunately, though, real estate's reputation among regular people is unduly pristine. In the west buying a home is akin to a rite of passage. It's a mark of success and a landmark of adulthood. Real estate is also coveted as a noble asset that "always goes up over time." While the 2008 financial meltdown should have defaced that theory, it is still widely held. As such, less educated investors and homeowners often purchase properties under the assumption that it must increase in value simply because it's real estate. They dangerously concentrate much of their personal wealth in their homes without understanding the risks involved.

As delightful as it would be, real estate is not a magical asset. It isn't destined to appreciate simply because it's tangible or because people can live in it. While it's true that real estate meets a fundamental human demand for shelter, that alone does not automatically guarantee profit. The fact is that it's an asset like any other. It can make an investor rich, provide flat returns or it can bankrupt a purchaser. There are countless elements that can determine the outcome of a real estate deal. I wrote this chapter to belie the divine praise it receives. Real estate is not only risky, but it's also complex. Here I'll outline five of the best ways to lose your money when buying real estate.

To begin, the first way to lose money in a real estate deal is to invest in a market with a declining population. To clarify, "population" can mean either people, businesses or both, depending on the type of property. With a receding net migration comes a lower demand for space and therefore a lesser requirement for real estate. As such, property values generally decline. A perfect example is the city of Detroit, which lost over half of its population between the 1950s and 2015. Real estate prices correspondingly fell. Today the average hovers around a mere $40,000; 50% of what it was eight years ago.

Of course, populations don't rise and fall without cause. Rather, they do so because of employment conditions. People move where there are jobs and they leave when those jobs disappear. Detroit is again a perfect example. While never a rich city by global standards, its rise in the first part of the 20th century and fall in the latter mirrored the American auto industry. The automobile business converged in Detroit in the early 1920s and brought with it thousands of manufacturing, managerial and executive jobs, as well creating spin-off employment in the legal, accounting, advisory and advertising industries. By the 1950s, however, the business began to decentralize from its hub in Detroit and jobs gradually escaped from the city. Thus began a gradual exodus and Detroit's population declined from over 1.8 million in 1950 to 714,000 today. Since populations typically ebb with receding employment, the second way to lose money in properties is to invest where jobs are not being created.

Another great way to destroy your portfolio is to misunderstand the type of property you're purchasing. Many investors make the error of thinking that all real estate is the same and thus set themselves up for failure. They believe that properties all react to the same economic elements, including the ones above. Instead, the asset class can be divided into a range of subsets. These include single-family homes, multifamily residential (apartment buildings), land development, land banking, industrial, agricultural, etc. Each type of real estate is impacted by a custom range of micro and macroeconomic factors.

For example, the value of a house is largely determined by two factors: how popular the area is to live in and how many buyers exist. It's a simple function of supply and demand. While some value can be added through renovations there is in fact little that can be done to control the price of a house. If a neighborhood becomes less desirable people will leave it. Or if the economy is weak there will be fewer purchasers on the market. In both cases housing prices will fall in spite of anything a homeowner does to preserve its worth.

Conversely, a poor economy can spur the growth of assets like apartment buildings. In post-2008 America these properties flourished due to a falling number of buyers and a growing amount of renters. As well, multifamily residential investors usually have more control over their properties' worth through rent price adjustments and renovations. Moreover, these buildings generally trade as assets independent of their competition. While a house wouldn't sell if it was twice the price of a comparable in the neighborhood, an apartment probably would if it produced twice the amount of profit than its competition. In essence, these assets trade as businesses. Thus, there is far more to understand about real estate fundamentals than simply considering whether a population is growing. Each subset of property comes with its own value-inducing factors.

Fourth, an investor can almost guarantee failure by investing in an overbuilt market. If areas look attractive for growth, developers may overshoot and produce too much inventory. As such, without looking at local housing starts, occupancy rates and relative price movement, investors run the risk of buying where there is too much of a real estate supply and not enough demand for it.

However, the prize of all money-losing strategies is to improperly study a deal's specifics before investing in it. The heart of every opportunity, real estate or otherwise, should be adequate due diligence. While a market may have an influx of migration, enormous job creation, plenty of good real estate locations and every other factor that would point to success, each opportunity is distinct from one another. For example, a property may be mispriced or perhaps the deal is poorly structured. Zoning permits may not be approved or costs could go beyond what was anticipated. There is no better way to wash out your money than to rely solely on market fundamentals and not on the investment's particulars.

Before adding real estate to your portfolio – and I also mean buying your own home – consider the above points. Too many people invest in the asset because they believe it will inevitably go up in value. Remember, real estate is no different than any asset: sometimes the deals are great and other times they're dreadful. The way to protect yourself is to perform thorough due diligence.

POSITION OF POWER

POSITION OF POWER

As I've mentioned in previous chapters, I accumulated a lot of my wealth by investing with borrowed funds. I'd frequently take out a loan, invest it into an asset and then use the earnings to pay down the principal and interest. The leftover cash was my profit. Over time, I borrowed enormous sums to magnify and maximize my returns.

In fact, using debt to invest was the bread and butter of my portfolio's early days. It allowed me to purchase assets that I otherwise couldn't afford and bolstered my passive income. With cheap interest rates and no shareholders to answer to, raising capital from lenders was a lucrative practice. Today, it's second nature to me.

In recent months, however, I've begun to reposition my strategy and recede from borrowing to invest. I've found that while many lenders, particularly large banks, promote themselves as supporters of small business and entrepreneurship, they are often also the first to call it quits when a venture appears to be in trouble. Rather than working with the entrepreneur, they prefer to mitigate their risk and cut the company out of their portfolio. For a small business, the result of being "cut out" by a bank usually means having a loan recalled just when they need it the most; the aftermath of which can be disastrous.

Of course, it's no surprise that big banks' priority is profit. Nobody is shocked to hear that small businesses are regularly burned by financial institutions. Last year, for example, one of my partners almost lost his building after a $1 million mortgage was recalled. He had never missed a payment, but the bank forced him to refinance unfavorably and almost cost him the real estate in which his employees worked.

In 2009 another of my associates, who financed commercial real estate developments, had a $10 million loan recalled suddenly and without notice. This automatically caused the project to stall and resulted in a $39 million loss for his investors. Frustratingly, the loan recall was unrelated to his project. Instead, his mortgage was swept up in a massive pool of broad call-ins during the financial crisis of that year. Recently, I had my own $300,000 scare, which forced me to scramble for that capital elsewhere.

The fact is that while banks are incredible sources of cheap and bountiful capital, their decision-makers are usually not entrepreneurs. As such, there's often a deep disconnect between the banks' interests and the business owners'. Entrepreneurs learn at the school of hard knocks and are used to roughing through peaks and valleys. We fully expect our ventures to take losses. We know that business is tumultuous. On the other hand, banking staff are typically corporate MBAs, CPAs and CFAs and get nervous when their borrowers get into trouble. While "getting into trouble" is part of what we do, it's also what causes bankers to pull the plug on us.

As such, if you intend to borrow funds to invest or do business, it's important to understand your lender's nature. Aside from what it claims in brochures and posters, how business-friendly is it really? Will your lender be there when – not if – your venture goes through its dark times? Or will it demand its money back when your financial position begins to sink, making it even harder for you to recover? What are the specific terms of the loan agreement beyond the interest rate and repayment date? Can it pull the plug on you at its leisure?

The lender's position of power is one of the most commonly-ignored risks of using leverage. In my opinion, cheap money is not always worth signing a contract that allows a bank to call in a loan without notice, without attempting to work with you and entirely at its discretion. I, myself, got caught in a mess because I took loans that placed me at the mercy of my banker.

Thus, while a bank is an important strategic capital partner to any entrepreneur, consider the terms of your relationship. If it isn't favorable, you may want to raise money from other sources. Mortgages and lines of credit aren't the only kinds of debt options, and borrowing funds isn't the only way to use leverage. For instance, you could offer equity in your company to private investors instead of approaching lenders.

There are indeed an assortment of ways to finance your venture, but the key is to learn the skills to do so. The ability to raise capital, not only efficiently but also legally and ethically, is perhaps an entrepreneur's most coveted tool. Knowing how to identify good and qualified investors can open the floodgates to private funds and decrease your reliance on a bank. If a lender knows that you have access to desirable capital elsewhere it cannot strong arm you into assuming a risky loan.

Furthermore, beyond seeking other capital sources, also consider diversifying your assets across financial institutions. Banks typically reserve the right to not only demand immediate repayment of loans at any time, but to also shut down your accounts without a warning or an explanation. From personal experience I can tell you that nothing can justify the administrative nightmare and stress that comes with moving your assets under the gun. I once made the mistake of completely trusting my bank, with which I had a 15-year relationship, and held all of my corporate, personal and even my wife's accounts with the same institution. Given my income, credit history and the fact that she was soon to become a doctor we saw little risk in doing so. To the contrary, our bank constantly solicited us for more business.

However, after years of rejecting its insurance and investment products and keeping little in savings, the bank apparently tired of our business. Two days before my wife's medical licensing exam, the most important test of her career, we were informed that all of our accounts were being terminated and were asked to repay a $300,000 line of credit in 21 days. After repeated unanswered calls to the bank and seeking guidance from our lawyer, we were eventually informed that it would not comment on its decision – and that it was final.

Thankfully, with every disaster comes a good lesson learned. We managed to come up with the funds and divided our accounts among a few different institutions to avoid a similar debacle. While the typical banking client likely has little to be concerned with, I know several entrepreneurs who faced an almost identical situation. In my view, the practicality of consolidating your accounts under one bank is simply not worth the risk.

Depending on how you do business a bank can either be your best friend or your worst enemy. To me, it's been both. While they're gushing with capital to lend and provide a secure means to store your cash, a soured attitude towards your business can lead to a catastrophic outcome. To be clear, I'm not suggesting that you disregard borrowing to invest. In fact, that can be one of the most lucrative ways to build wealth. Instead, my point is to be cognizant of the terms and conditions of the loans you take. Remember that financial institutions are companies that serve their shareholders. As such, they'll do what they must in order to earn their investors a profit. Banks work for them – not for us – so be cautious of your relationship.

WHY MOST PEOPLE WILL NEVER BE WEALTHY

WHY MOST PEOPLE WILL NEVER BE WEALTHY

As much as I'd like this book to be a positive one, the reality is that most people will never be financially free. The chips are stacked too highly against the average person for him to easily succeed. Instead, the majority in the west will live a life entirely dependent on employment income. Once they retire and lose their salary, they will be forced to downsize, reduce costs and supplement their meagre savings with government assistance. Their portfolios, assuming they even have them, will do little, if anything, to benefit them. That is the fate of most in the developed world. In this final chapter I'll address two of the greatest financial roadblocks that most people will face. I'll also offer what I believe is the best solution to them all.

1. Our Education System Ignores Wealth Management

Like many other places, North America's education system does not teach wealth management. While schools offer courses like Physical Education, Art,

Cooking and Woodworking, the majority of people endure 15 years of education without even learning the basics of a credit card. Topics like saving, home ownership, entrepreneurship, investing and insurance are ignored altogether.

Students thus move from elementary, high school, post-secondary and then graduate to become income-earning young adults with zero financial knowledge. They want to make money and understand that it's important, but they don't know where to begin. To most, the seemingly obvious place to go to for advice is their bank. They then go on to take out six-figure mortgages, lines of credit, they purchase insurance policies and make investments – all without the skills to know if what they're doing is in fact beneficial. And so begins a dangerous spiral.

Case in point is my own wife, Elisa, who spent the better part of a decade studying to become a doctor. Between 36-hour shifts at the hospital and writing exams there was little time for her to learn about money management. As with many of her colleagues she never thought much about building wealth.

However, since they day I've known Elisa I've watched bankers, insurance and mutual fund salesmen badger her for her business. They offer her lunch, they sponsor her events and they email and call her frequently to pitch every product under the sun. A financial advisor once even contacted Elisa's mother to inquire why her daughter won't return his messages.

Of course, these industry professionals are smart. They prey on the fact that the longer one stays in school the less time they have to learn about building wealth. They know that the education system won't teach its students about money, and doctors in particular will emerge as financially-illiterate large income earners. What better client is there to have?

It's no surprise then that many North Americans live paycheque to paycheque. After servicing their monthly expenses they have absolutely no cash left to save or invest. Most submerge deeper into debt. In fact, people's financial futures here are generally quite bleak. The average Canadian household's debt is over 160% of its disposable income. In the US, 15% of seniors live in poverty and most in both countries will require government financial assistance at some point in their lives. A 2015 HSBC survey showed that the majority of Canadians will never fully retire because their portfolios and federal pension plans combined aren't enough for them to live adequately on.

The reality is that North Americans don't learn the skills necessary to even stay solvent, let alone to become wealthy. This is a serious failure not only on the parts of governments, schools, colleges and universities – but also on society in general. Pupils believe that the sole purpose of school is to study, aim for university and one day become employed. And just like their parents, these children will grow up to be paycheque addicts whose sole source of sustenance is the salary determined by their bosses. There is little emphasis in school on entrepreneurship and even less on investing.

Ironically, wealth is not built through employment. Instead, it's done by investing and building businesses - the same two categories ignored by the education system. Schools pre-program their students to become job-dependent instead of financially independent. They manufacture employees instead of giving students a fair opportunity to explore other options, thus limiting their chances to build wealth. From day one, they set them up for failure.

Strangely enough, we as a society attribute entrepreneurship to a certain type of personality. It's commonly said that most are simply not designed to be risk-takers or business owners. Entrepreneurs are painted as a rare breed of risk-taking outliers with an appetite for adventure. Most people would just prefer the comfort a stable job, and that's why they'll never be rich.

Perhaps, though, it isn't that a mere few are inherently supposed to be business owners. Maybe it's not about personalities. Is it much of a stretch to suggest that we find entrepreneurship less attractive because the people who teach us encourage employment over entrepreneurship? Could it conceivably be that our failure to promote business ownership and investing to students as the clearest path to financial freedom results in their ignorance of that concept? What if we encouraged our children not to study hard to become employees, but to study hard to be employers? Instead of glamorizing the corporate ladder climb, what if we told students that owning a business or being an investor was the surest way to become rich, respected, free and independent? If we shifted the way we educate would we see a spike in entrepreneurship? We absolutely would.

The greatest paradox of all is that it's extremely easy to start a business in North America. A company can be created with just a few clicks on a laptop and there are all kinds of tax incentives for doing so. Our market is free, fair, sensibly-regulated and is bursting with opportunities. And thanks to the internet it has never been cheaper or easier to do business here. With low barriers to entry and plenty of money to be made, Canada and the US are starving for new entrepreneurs and investors.

Thus, while our education system should prepare the next generation for the future, it's actually a handicap to wealth creation. Students could graduate from school excited to build companies, invest, be entrepreneurs, create jobs, take risks and have a real shot at becoming multimillionaires. Those who opt to pursue employment could also do well for themselves by astutely managing their income and investments. Instead, however, it mostly produces employees who are too uneducated to make good financial decisions.

2. Our Investment Market is Prohibitive

Canada and the US are home to a plethora of outstanding investment opportunities. With world-class infrastructure, stable governments, diverse economies and coveted resource, finance, energy and real estate markets, they attract hundreds of billions of dollars in foreign capital each year. There are countless lucrative ventures here, including oil drilling, mining, commercial real estate, technology firms, auto dealerships, apartment buildings, agricultural production and lending to name only a short few.

As I write this chapter from my condo in Vancouver, I'm surrounded by dozens of tall and glamorous-looking commercial and residential buildings. Most could accommodate a couple of hundred tenants and, if I could guess, would likely have cost in the range of $20-60 million to build. Vancouver has one of the world's most lucrative real estate markets and I'm sure that the investors in those deals did quite well for themselves.

The question to consider, though, is which investors financed these commercial developments? Who was fortunate enough to participate in the profits of constructing, selling or leasing these units in Canada's prime real estate market? The answer is simple: private equity firms, high net-worth individuals, investment funds, companies and institutional investors. Or more specifically, not the average Canadian.

The reality is that many of the most lucrative investments are privately-owned enterprises. Whether they're land development ventures, energy plays, large-scale commercial real estate or otherwise, opportunities of this nature often trounce the returns available in stocks and mutual funds. And unfortunately they're reserved for only three kinds of investors:

1. Sophisticated investors

2. Wealthy investors

3. Well-connected investors

Of course, this is no conspiracy; it's just a fact. The biggest and most lucrative investments are simply not available to the retail investor. For instance, the average person is typically not invited to invest in a $200 million private real estate deal. Joe American doesn't receive phone calls to partake in the next big 3,000 acre land development. However, somebody obviously does because those projects exist across the country. And that somebody is a person or company with a lot of money: corporate, institutional and high net worth investors.

Conversely, most people get little more than an annual email from a mutual fund salesperson suggesting that they contribute to their retirement accounts. They're mostly limited to traditional investments like stocks and bonds. In fact, the majority of North Americans have never, and will never, participate in anything other than what their bank offers them. The only kind of real estate they'll ever buy is their own house.

As I mentioned, it's neither surreptitious nor mysterious why the wealthy have access to better investment opportunities. Instead, it is the way it is for three main reasons:

1. The rich are better connected than most.

2. The rich can afford to make bigger investments.

3. Governments restrict the investments that the average person can make.

I'll illustrate the first two points by using a couple of examples.

Henry the Carpenter

Henry is a carpenter in Calgary. He earns $25 an hour and works long days to make a living. He is married with two young children. Henry takes pride in what he does, but he also knows that his job isn't going to make him rich. Instead, he has to focus on investing to create wealth for his family. He knows that if he buys enough income-producing assets he'll earn enough revenue to be financially free – so that's what he sets out to do.

In spite of what everyone he knows does, Henry doesn't want to invest with the bank. He used to own mutual funds, but he sold them months ago because they never did as well as his financial advisor said they would. In fact, after the constant ups and downs of the market, he doesn't even know if they ever made a profit.

This time, though, Henry's going to play it differently. He's going to be smarter about how he invests and instead follow what wealthy people do. After his own experience with mutual funds and recognizing that the rich don't invest in them, he knows where he's going to put his capital now: into a private deal. Henry has $40,000 in his RRSP retirement account and he's ready to put it to use.

After reading in the news that business in Calgary is growing, Henry believes that commercial real estate developments could be a great place to invest. He thinks that the city's downtown will expand rapidly and that he should invest in an A-grade high-rise building. After all, that type of real estate would probably be in demand if the business boom continues.

Unfortunately, Henry doesn't know any real estate developers that could undertake a project of that size. Some of his friends have done condo-conversions and built houses, but nothing much bigger than that. Nobody in his network is especially wealthy and most of them don't think much about investing anyway. Without any contacts, Henry doesn't even know where to begin.

Instead of giving up, though, Henry searches online for Calgary's biggest real estate developers. Eventually, he finds a company called Calgary Capital and visits their website. Online, he can see the calibre of buildings the firm constructed in the past. Many are over 40 floors tall with beautiful reflective glass frames. They must be worth millions of dollars.

Since this is exactly what he's been looking for, Henry calls the firm. He speaks to a receptionist, who then passes him on to a gentleman in client relations. Henry explains to the man that he has $40,000 in his RRSP to invest in Calgary Capital's next deal and wants to book an appointment to discuss it further.

The man on the other line chuckles and says, "Sorry, sir. Our projects usually cost $110 million to develop. We don't accept investments of less than $3 million. And our buildings aren't RRSP eligible." He hangs up the phone.

Marcy the Forestry Entrepreneur

Marcy just returned from vacation. She had previously spent three weeks in Barbados with 16 of her family members to celebrate the successful sale of her business, Lumber Management and Trading, to a major New York Stock Exchange-listed company. After taxes, she made over $34 million on the sale.

With all of this cash on hand, Marcy decides to invest it in real estate. There's no sense in keeping it in the bank. While she doesn't have a lot of experience in buying properties, she has plenty of friends who do. In fact, one of her lawyer's clients, Bryan, owns a firm in Calgary called Calgary Capital, the city's most prominent real estate developer.

Marcy talks to her lawyer, who then arranges for her to meet with Bryan the next week. Her lawyer made a lot of money on the sale of Marcy's business too, and wants to keep her happy. At their appointment, she informs Bryan that she just sold her company and is looking for real estate to invest in.

Bryan explains to Marcy that most of his developments are in the $100 million range. He is currently building high-rises in Calgary because he thinks that's where Canada's next commercial real estate boom will be. His next development is a 42-floor building called "The Grandeur" that is primed for major companies to move into. In fact, he has already pre-sold several floors to a Russian oil-drilling firm.

The Grandeur will cost $92 million to develop. Bryan's business plan is similar to most of his other projects. Calgary Capital will secure a $55 million loan from two banks that he's worked with in the past. The remaining funds will come from investors—a combination of pension funds, private equity firms and individuals who can invest a minimum of $3 million.

Marcy explains to Bryan that she's heard great things about his developments. But, she'll need to do some due diligence before she decides to invest in The

Grandeur. She's never done a deal like this and wants to make sure that her capital is protected. After all, an investment of this calibre is not simply about guessing whether the price of real estate will go up or down. It requires years of planning, zoning, legal contacts, microeconomic analysis and contact with the local government.

The next week, Marcy calls a meeting with her closest advisors. She directs them to hire a team of attorneys, accountants, realtors and CFAs to analyze The Grandeur's prospects. She also consults several of her friends who made their money in real estate. As well, since the local government had a stake in her lumber business she knows several of Calgary's politicians quite well. She invites three of them for dinner at her home and asks for their opinions.

After two months, Marcy spent a total of $40,000 in legal and accounting fees. However, the cost is well worth it because her team advised her to make the investment. In fact, with a projected annualized return of 25 per cent, The Grandeur's prospects are so attractive that she decides to invest $5 million.

The Differences between Henry and Marcy

The above examples illustrate that the regular investor is at a serious disadvantage when compared to the rich. Henry was well ahead of most people because he understood that wealth is not created through employment. Rather, it's done through prudent investing. He also recognized that there are better assets out there than what the banks offer. He even pinpointed what he considered to be the most lucrative opportunity in Calgary. However, when he attempted to make the investment he was promptly rejected.

Henry, a man who earns roughly the average North American's salary, had neither the connections nor the money to invest in a project like The Grandeur. None of his friends were rich, few took investing seriously and he had nobody there to guide him. His retirement account was useless to a private investment and he certainly didn't have $3 million.

On the other hand, Marcy had ample money to invest in The Grandeur. Even though she wasn't an experienced or sophisticated investor, she had contacts in her network who could help her. Marcy was also able to spend tens of thousands of dollars on due diligence before investing $5 million. As such, she got access to one of the best opportunities in all of Calgary.

Of course, not all investments can be painted with the same brush. Just because a deal is bigger does not mean that it is better. As well, real estate or private opportunities don't always equal profit. There are certainly bad ones out there. However, I'll ask you this: in general, would you rather invest in a bank's mutual fund or in a development similar to The Grandeur?

Most people would likely prefer the latter. However,

99% of them will never have the opportunity to invest in a deal of that calibre. They have neither the net worth nor the network needed to do so. Therefore, they're left with what their investment advisor offers: stocks, bonds and mutual funds.

Government Regulation

As noted, there are three reasons for why most North Americans are excluded from the most lucrative opportunities – the first two I illustrated above. The third is that governments have made it nearly impossible for regular people to participate in large, private opportunities like The Grandeur.

In both Canada and the US, laws divide investors into two primary categories: accredited (rich) and retail (normal). While accredited investors are largely ignored by regulators, securities commissions in both countries discourage retail investors from buying assets aside from stocks, bonds and mutual funds. Again, this is not a conspiracy; it's for their own protection.

Unfortunately, the business world is home to many scammers and crooked characters. It's not just a glossy place where jobs and wealth are created. There are certainly bad apples. For example, in 2012 over $1 billion was embezzled in fraudulent investment deals in Alberta, alone. Thousands of people fall victim to deceit each year and they are usually unexperienced, mom-and-pop investors.

The challenge with investing is that it isn't always easy to perform adequate due diligence. Thoroughly assessing the viability of a business takes a requisite level of sophisticated skill and knowledge. Everything from its legal structure, financial position, management capability and execution potential must be considered. Of course, if a wealthy person isn't confident in an investment, he always can hire lawyers, analysts and accountants to assist with his research before committing his capital. He has the resources to ensure that every element of the deal checks out. And if the investment fails, he probably has enough wealth to sustain the loss.

However, the regular Canadian or American does not have the same ability. Thanks to the failings of our education system, he lacks the skills to acutely analyse the prospects of an investment and certainly cannot afford to lose his money. With neither business acumen, financial cushioning nor realistic access to help, he's therefore far more susceptible to bad deals, scams and money-losing ventures.

Governments recognize this disparity and thus seek to protect retail investors by restricting their eligibility to participate in most opportunities. In Canada and the US, for example, they are generally only allowed to place their funds into government bonds, mutual funds or with companies that trade on the stock market. These assets are subjected to intense regulation, disclosure and reporting and are simpler to perform due diligence on. Non-approved companies and individuals are prohibited from raising capital from the general public. That's why a bank can offer you an investment into a mutual fund, but not in a local business.

The result of such regulation is that most investment opportunities, both good and bad, are removed from the majority's radar. While this likely does limit fraud, it also precludes the average investor from ever participating in some of the best deals. For example, even if Calgary Capital was willing to accept Henry's $40,000 investment, unless it was licensed with the government (which is an entirely separate can of worms), it would not have been allowed to. Thus, the rich receive exclusive access to the private market and they continue to get wealthier. The rest are left with second-class investments that are offered by banks and mutual fund companies.

What Needs to Change

The formula for access to the best investments is simple: become a sophisticated investor with high financial literacy, an entrepreneurial spirit and a great network. Or, be rich.

While society frequently ponders North America's economic future, we never actually address the root problem: our complete absence of investment and business knowledge. The average person knows little more about money than the balance on his credit card. As such, I wonder if we'd have the same amount of household and sovereign debt, low incomes and disenfranchised portions of our population if people knew more about wealth management. If regular investors could earn twice as much profit as they currently do, would they be in a better financial position? If marginalized and low-income people knew that their path towards financial independence was entrepreneurship – not working for minimum wage – would they benefit? How much better would life be if we all knew more about building wealth?

Federal spending cuts, tax increases and budget changes are all short-term solutions to economic stimulation. They only exist to plug holes. In my opinion, the only way to truly improve the quality of life for all people is through better financial education. With that said, I'm unconfident that our overall financial literacy will ever improve. While you may opt to take action independently (and I hope you do), North America as a whole will doubtfully take strides forward. Broadly increasing financial literacy is a quagmire for several reasons.

First, systematic changes are often made on a political level. Whether it's with local or national governments or with provincial/state education boards, there needs to be some sort of lobbying for the issue to gain traction. Unfortunately, unlike environmentalists or human rights groups, there are no prominent organizations picketing for increased financial literacy. Nobody important is rallying elected officials to encourage schools to teach wealth management. As such, policymakers are uncompelled to take action on the subject.

I won't speculate too much on why this is the case, but I will sneak in a brief hypothesis here. Personally, I think that North Americans don't know just how uneducated they are about their finances. To most, earning a mediocre return on investment, having plenty of debt and relying on government assistance for retirement is the norm; they don't expect much more. We generally don't realize that there's a problem and are therefore not motivated to make a change.

Second, it's hard to educate society about a subject that is far from absolute. Wealth management encompasses a range of diverse opinions and is not an exact science. There are few right or wrong answers. For example, some, like me, believe that owning a home that you live in (as opposed to renting it to a tenant) is a poor decision for most people to make. Others believe that it's the best possible investment. One bestselling author believes that mutual funds are terrible purchases and another wrote his entire book to promote them. There's little consensus on the subject. Who is anyone, including me, to say that their approach to achieving financial goals is correct?

Third, the wealth management business is a multibillion-dollar industry dominated by a few key companies. It doesn't take an imaginative leap to assume that major financial institutions would object to society questioning the status quo. I doubt that banks would take kindly to a plethora of North Americans rejecting mutual funds, RRSPs and Roth IRAs, or even simply reducing their reliance on professional wealth management services. For better or for worse, financial institutions yield tremendous power. Unless they benefit from it, they likely will attempt to block any real change.

Lastly, a major transformation would probably require involvement with regulatory bodies like the securities commissions. A more financially educated populous might demand easy access to investments outside the scope of traditional stocks, bonds and mutual funds. More Canadians and Americans may seek private or alternative investment opportunities or even try to structure their own deals, thus venturing into territory that regulators are less comfortable with. They would likely need ample time to adapt to a changing investment environment.

As such, while I'd love to see a systematic overhaul I doubt that it will ever happen. There are too many obstacles standing in the way. Instead, I'd like to propose the following as a small step in the right direction: education boards should implement a class about the financial markets, entrepreneurship, banking and business as a core part of the school curriculum. A course of this nature should rank as highly as mathematics and sciences.

This would not be a wealth management class. Instead, it would teach concrete, black-and-white information about what banks are, how the stock market works, what mortgages are, how credit functions and how monetary policy is decided, etc. In the same way that History class teaches about great explorers and military generals, this would teach students about our most coveted entrepreneurs, like Bill Gates or Steve Jobs. It would not push on them a certain ideology. It would not make recommendations. Instead, it would simply give students the information they need to one day draw their own conclusions about money, business and wealth management.

In my opinion, even rudimentary knowledge about how our financial system works would be a major improvement. A more educated society would be less susceptible to scams, poor investments and deceptive salespeople. We'd likely take on less bad debt and think twice about making decisions based on "what you're supposed to do." We as a people would benefit as a whole.

Of course, as much as one can dream I doubt that anything close to my meagre suggestion will ever occur. Instead, change needs to take place at the grassroots level with people like you. If I can give one piece of advice, it would be this: get your financial education from a broad range of people. Consider all opinions and discover as much as you can. Be open-minded and over time shape your own strategies and methods. Most importantly, however, treat your financial education as seriously as you would anything else important. In the same way that athletes don't expect to make the big leagues unless they practice for thousands of hours or doctors won't practice unless they've had a decade of study, how can you expect to get rich without devoting yourself to the craft?

You are solely responsible for your financial future. Take control of it now.

ABOUT THE AUTHOR

Alexis Assadi is a venture capital investor who built his wealth in his mid-20s by investing with entrepreneurs. To date, he has financed nearly 50 small businesses through his company, Assadi Global Ventures, Inc. Alexis has lived in Australia, Hong Kong, Switzerland, Thailand and the United States. He graduated from Saint George's School in Vancouver and received a Bachelor of Arts in Political Science from the University of British Columbia. In 2011 he was honorarily inducted into the Golden Keys International Honours Society by the University of Victoria.

Alexis enjoys spending time with his family and friends. He's particularly fond of frequenting sushi restaurants and steakhouses with them, albeit that's mostly because someone else is paying. He loves good conversation over whiskey and cigars, wristwatches, funny videos on the internet and great comedians. Alexis lives in Vancouver with his wife, Elisa, and their bunny, Pepper.

Visit him online at www.Alexis Assadi.net

CPSIA information can be obtained at www.ICGtesting.com
Printed in the USA
BVOW01s1457300716

457039BV00007B/165/P